AskMen.com

PRESENTS

THE
STYLE BIBLE

THE 11 RULES FOR BUILDING
A COMPLETE AND
TIMELESS WARDROBE

EDITED BY JAMES BASSIL

Collins

An Imprint of HarperCollinsPublishers

Contributors:

Chris Rovny
Maggie Kalogeropoulos
Jonathan Sandals
Farah Averill
Daniel Harrison
Karin Eldor
Alex Muniz
Jarrid Adler
Suzy Small
Sal Ciolfi
Norma McHenry
Daniel J. Indiviglio
Adam Di Stefano

Interior illustrations: Amy Boehmer and Pamela Kenny (amyboehmer@gmail.com, pam.kenny@gmail.com)

HarperCollins books may be purchased for educational, business, or sales promotional use. For information, please write: Special Markets Department, HarperCollins Publishers, 10 East 53rd Street, New York, NY 10022.

FIRST EDITION

Designed by Jaime Putorti

Library of Congress Cataloging-in-Publication Data

Askmen.com presents the style bible : the 11 rules for building a complete and timeless wardrobe / edited by James Bassil.—1st ed.
        p.   cm.
    Includes index.
    ISBN: 978-0-06-120850-8
    1. Men's clothing. 2. Men's furnishing goods. 3. Fashion. I. Bassil, James.
II. AskMen.com. III. Title: Style bible.
    TT617.A75 2007
    646'.32—DC22

                                                2007016746

07 08 09 10 11 WST/QW 10 9 8 7 6 5 4 3 2 1

AskMen.com

PRESENTS

THE
STYLE BIBLE

Also Available from AskMen.com:

AskMen.com Presents From the Bar to the Bedroom

CONTENTS

RULE 10: MAINTAIN YOUR WARDROBE   177

RULE 11: GROOMING   193

INTRODUCTION

As boys, we are taught that masculinity and a concern for style are incompatible. Fashion is the domain of the woman, and too early an immersion in it might put us on the path to becoming sissies. This idea is hammered into us by our fathers and friends throughout childhood and adolescence, typically until we reach our early twenties. Then, an abrupt and complete reversal in philosophy is thrust upon us. Suddenly, "image is everything," "shoes make the man," and "women love a well-dressed man." We set out on scrambled shopping trips to get ourselves up to date, but, with no acquired style savvy to steer us, we mistakenly let ourselves be guided only by price tags and our favorite colors. The unhappy result? A generation of men that spends too much money on clothes that don't look good on them.

Clearly, this is not a sustainable state of affairs. We need to remedy it. Now, we're not about to suggest that men set about raising their sons differently, because we think we're generally doing a good job at that. What we will do, however, is provide males with the information that they need to make it through that troubling transition from not knowing how to dress to knowing how to dress.

How do we know what information you need? Well, at AskMen.com, we've been receiving your style-related questions for years now. Every day, we're hit with e-mails asking how long pants should be, what appropriate office wear is, and how to match that shirt with those pants. In fact, the volume and variety of your style queries is rivaled only by that of your sex queries (and you send us a lot of sex queries). So we've had plenty of direction in assembling the first and last fashion book you'll ever need: AskMen.com's *Style Bible*.

The 11 rules that comprise the *Style Bible* will take you through every step in assembling the complete male wardrobe. We know that you are not interested in boring historical backgrounds, so we will stick to the practical, functional advice: the tips that you will be able to apply immediately so that you can begin to enjoy the benefits of this book before you even finish reading it. And by the time you have closed the back cover, you may want to learn more, but you will not need to. Your closet will be stocked full of all the clothes you need, all of which will fit and flatter you perfectly. Women will notice this. You will have the knowledge to replenish that closet when the time comes. And you will have saved yourself a bundle in the process, having spared yourself from future useless trial-and-error purchases.

In short, you will save money and impress women. Only good will come of reading this book. So let's not delay ourselves any further. We'll start with the primary rule of dressing well: dressing for oneself.

AskMen.com

PRESENTS

THE

STYLE BIBLE

RULE 1
KNOW YOURSELF

In the world of popular culture, fashion is almost always displayed against the canvas of other people. *What* is considered current or trendy is invariably a question of *who* is wearing it, whether that who is a model on a foreign runway or a celeb on television. In this climate, it's easy to lose sight of the fact that true style resides in accommodating individuality, rather than blindly following the lead of others.

That last phrase has become something of a cliché, but one worthy of reexamination because it is so commonly misread. When we speak of individuality in fashion, we're not referring to using one's wardrobe as a means to showcase one's independence (by, for example, wearing purple snakeskin boots as a fierce declaration of your free-thinking ways). Nor are we referring to eschewing popular trends simply because they are popular. What we are advocating is the simple act of setting oneself as the primary criterion in dictating what one wears. In other words, don't wear the color purple because everyone in London or Milan is wearing purple. Wear the color purple because you've researched what colors match your skin type and the rest of your wardrobe, and purple came out near the top of the list.

Getting to know yourself in a style sense is not an overnight process.

It takes time and experimentation and you will make plenty of mistakes along the way. But the rewards are many. The man who is conscious of his own style walks with confidence, because he knows that his garments do not look awkward on him. His shopping excursions are much less exasperating than those of other men, because he knows exactly what suits him and does not need to waste his time discovering as much through dressing room trial and error. And his wardrobe is perfectly streamlined: devoid of those orphan garments that are worn once and then never again, and filled with clothes that will prove useful for years to come. And his bank account is all the healthier for it.

Your first step toward becoming that man consists in determining the style of clothes that best suit your physical body type.

DRESS RIGHT FOR YOUR BODY TYPE

Although Thomas Jefferson decreed that "all men are created equal," when it comes to body type and clothing, that bold statement is simply untrue. Knowing how to dress for your body type as well as which styles to avoid is the key to honing your personal style.

One thing to always keep in mind when shopping for new clothes is that the fit of the garment is its ultimate test. If an expensive jacket just isn't right for your body, it's going to look bad no matter what the price tag. Conversely, a cheaper jacket that accentuates your assets and disguises the things you don't love about yourself will make you look like a million bucks even without a million-dollar price tag. So to learn about how to dress for your body type, how to find the clothes that are most flattering for you, and how to avoid the most common body-type faux pas men make, read on.

The Bulky Man

- *Buy clothes that fit trimly*

Many bulkier fellows mistakenly believe that tight clothing will smother imperfections and flatten out pudgy shapes. However, tight clothing will only draw attention to your flabby bits. In a similar vein, other plus-size men believe baggy clothing will hide bulges. Not so. Overly large clothes will only make you look even bigger. The secret to looking slimmer is to choose clothes that are neither tight nor baggy, meaning that all your clothes should just skim your body without hugging it too closely.

THE LARGER MAN: TIPS FOR A GOOD FIT

■ Avoid any sweater, blazer, or shirt with naturally sloped shoulders because these tend to attract the eye right down to your mid-section.

■ Jackets should be well adjusted around your waist area and should fall right below your buttocks.

■ Trousers should be worn on your hips, preferably with a low-rise, which is a shorter distance between the top of the waistband and the crotch of your pants.

■ Avoid letting your belly stick out over your pants; this lengthens your torso and shortens your legs, resulting in a very unattractive combination.

- *Stay away from horizontal stripes*

If there's a little more of you to love, particularly in the stomach area, avoid any kind of horizontal stripe. While you're at it, avoid diagonal stripes too. Both draw attention to the span of your chest. What you should wear with pride, however, are shirts and trousers with vertical stripes. Vertical stripes draw the eye downward, elongating your silhouette and visually slimming it. Pinstripe suits are the perfect dress-up clothes for you, especially paired with a crisp black dress shirt underneath. Pinstripe dress shirts will also look great when mixed with dark jeans or black trousers. For casual wear, try to find a pair of dark corduroys with slim stripes that are made from thin material.

• *Go monochromatic*

A shirt and trousers in two extremely contrasting colors—like black and white—will break you in half and make a large middle stand out. Choose tops and bottoms that are identical or similar in color to create a cleaner visual impression and to look ten pounds slimmer instantly. And, of course, choose all black for the most slimming effect, but add some colored accessories to avoid looking like you have a funeral to attend.

• *Choose prints carefully*

Unless you're on a drunken adventure through Hawaii, stay away from T-shirts or dress shirts with large or busy prints if you're a bulky guy. These kinds of prints will draw attention to the upper half of your body, which is especially bad if you have a large belly that you would like to conceal. Obviously, printed shirts add flair to a wardrobe, so you shouldn't swear them off entirely. You'll look best in a shirt with a small print that is spaced quite far apart.

• *Avoid turtlenecks*

If you are heavy-set, avoid turtlenecks at all costs and opt instead for V-neck T-shirts, long-sleeve tops, and sweaters. This type of collar draws the eye down with the effect of creating a sleeker silhouette. In addition, a V-neck will give you the illusion of having a longer neck, particularly if you have a short neck or a double chin.

• *Minimize excess weight*

Bulky wool sweaters, for example, will add undesired volume to your waist and chest. Instead, opt for lighter fabrics such as cotton, linen, or thinner blends of wool and synthetic fibers.

• *Avoid double-vented jackets*

The slits in the back of your jacket are referred to as "vents." If you have a larger behind that makes you feel a bit self-conscious, stay away from blazers and jackets that are double-vented (the ones with two slits in the back) as this cut will draw attention to your posterior. To camouflage a wider rear, opt for a nicely fitted single-breasted blazer, preferably one that can be buttoned all the way up. The higher buttons will help divert people's attention from the area between your waist and chest.

- *Slacks*

If you're a rotund individual, try not to wear tight or baggy pants. When buying pants, a good fit is essential. Also, try to avoid pants with pleats, as they'll make your pelvic area look bigger.

The idea is to make your stems look longer rather than wider. If your belly sticks out, consider wearing suspenders under your blazer, thereby removing the visual spotlight from your midriff.

- *Wear a belt*

A belt will nip in your waistline and make it appear slimmer. Just be sure not to make it so tight that your belly hangs over it.

- *Lighten up*

Empty unnecessary items from your pockets; overstuffed pockets also call attention to your mid-section.

The Tall and Skinny Man
- *Choose fitted shirts*

Loose-fitting, untucked shirts will billow around you and make you look like the mainsail on a mast, so you'll want to choose something more fitted instead. While you should avoid skintight shirts because they will accentuate your bony upper half, do choose slim-cut shirts and learn how to layer them to fake a bit more mass. Always make sure your top fits comfortably around your chest and shoulders.

THE THIN MAN: TIPS FOR A GOOD FIT

■ Make sure most of your tops don't mold to your waistline. Instead, look for garments with a bit of contour to add volume to your midsection.

■ Whether you wear single or double-breasted blazers, make sure to adjust them so they fit properly throughout your entire body. Avoid any baggy areas under the arms or in the shoulder area.

■ To avoid looking like a lollipop, don't wear blazers or jackets with big shoulder pads.

■ Make sure all your jackets fall right under your buttocks. A shorter jacket will emphasize your height as well as your skinny waist, arms, and legs. A longer jacket, on the other hand, can make you look like a blanket-covered stick (not very appealing, especially when it's windy).

■ Your pants should be worn over your hips. Also, be sure to wear high-rise (a longer distance between the crotch of your pants and the top of the waistband) pants.

● *Avoid monochromatic looks*

If you wear a solid color from head to toe (especially black), you'll seem even thinner than you are, so break up your look by wearing a few different colors in your outfit. Fortunately, playing around with the color palette should be fun and you'll get to experiment with a lot of different looks.

● *Choose lighter colors*

Lighter colors will make you appear slightly larger, so choose whites, creams, light blues, light grays, and pastels to visually bulk you up a bit.

● *Don't wear vertical stripes*

No woman wants a man who looks like he's withering away, so if you're tall and thin, choose horizontal stripes to bulk you up a bit. A single, large horizontal stripe across the chest area can be particularly flattering because it will make your shoulders appear broader and will make you look like you have a better physique. You can also choose horizontal glen checks (we'll explain what these are later) to help you look a little meatier.

- ## *Avoid round-toed shoes*

If you're really tall, shoes with a round toe will make you look disproportionate. To balance out your shape, go for square-toed or pointy shoes. When it comes to dress shoes and city shoes, finding these styles should not present a problem. If you're at the gym or playing a sport, however, they will be harder to find, so just avoid anything with an overly round shape.

- ## *Stay away from skinny jeans*

The anorexic female model/'80s rocker look is never a flattering one for a man, so just say no to skinny jeans. Your pants should have a classic cut and should remain simple. A straight-cut or boot-cut jean with a long inseam will flatter you best.

Don't be afraid to wear pants with various motifs, lines, and patterns because these add volume. Another way to add volume: try pants with pleats around the pockets. Cuffs can also give the illusion that you have beefy legs, and well-fitted corduroy pants help to yield the "beefed-up" legs look.

The Short Man

- ## *A proper fit is key*

Above all, it's important that your clothes fit flawlessly. Looser garments can make you look stumpy, so opt for a fit that is trim rather than baggy. Jackets and blazers should fall slightly below your buttocks.

- ## *Wear one color*

Wearing a shirt and pants in the same color will prevent obvious breaks in your natural frame, and as a result can produce the illusion of height.

- *Opt for dark shades and light fabrics*

Dark colors, especially black, tend to have a slimming effect and help shorter men seem more elongated. The same applies to light or medium-weight fabrics. Heavier fabrics, on the other hand, tend to make you look bulkier and shorter.

- *Wear vertical stripes*

Anything that elongates your height is a good thing. For example, vertical stripes in clothing can help extend the look of your shorter body. Patterns such as pinstripe, chalkstripe, and herringbone also offer that "vertical" effect.

TIP-TOP TIPS

■ Avoid wearing blazers or cardigans with more than three buttons; these are designed for taller men and will make you look shorter.

■ V-neck T-shirts and sweaters will make your torso look longer.

■ Avoid tucking in baggy tops because they will make you look like an ice cube (wide and short).

- *Opt for square-toed shoes*

Pointy-toe shoes work when you're taller and your pant leg can cover most of your shoe. If you are smaller, however, long shoes or really big, bulky ones will make you look less like a professional and more like a joker. Square-toe shoes are best for you.

- *Wear heels on your shoes*

Although you should avoid wearing overly bulky shoes, you should buy shoes with a substantial heel. Dress boots are a great option for shorter men, and there are so many great styles available nowadays that can be paired with everything from jeans to a suit. To really give yourself added height, wear your dress boots with a longer pant leg that comes to the floor to disguise the heel.

Be careful, though; platforms or thick soles aren't always the best way to make short men look taller. Teetering is never in style, and an unnaturally high heel can make you look like you're insecure and uncomfortable with your smaller body structure.

- *Consider accessories*

Clever accessories, like a great necklace, tie, or hat, can keep people's eyes on your face, making them less likely to pay attention to your stature. Of all your accessory choices, a hat is probably best as it is a fantastic way to provide the illusion of an extra inch or two of height. And by hat, we don't mean a formfitting beanie. Try a newsboy cap for a trendier look.

- *Avoid really big prints*

On smaller bodies, giant prints will overwhelm. Keep your prints proportionate to your body; i.e., choose smaller prints, like micro-checks.

- *Wear a small rise*

The rise in your pants is the distance between the crotch of your pants and the waistband. Shorter men should wear the smallest rise in their pants that they can get away with because a really long rise will make you look like you have a negative butt, as well as make what you've got in front look nonexistent. In contrast, a short rise will visually elongate your legs and avoid making your crotch and bottom area look baggy and empty.

It's also wise to avoid any kind of puckering around the hips caused by full pockets, or tight and badly designed pants. They will make you look wider.

- *Choose a slimmer necktie*

Slim to medium-sized neckties won't overwhelm a more diminutive frame. Large ties should be avoided, because they will make your body seem disproportionate by comparison. If you are very short, you might want to check out ties that are both slimmer and shorter.

TALLER TIPS

Three simple yet often overlooked tips that can help you appear taller:

1. Maintaining good posture is key if you want to hit your maximum height potential. Remember to sit with your back straight and stand proud with your head up high at all times. A slouched stance will only make you look shorter, not to mention insecure.

2. Keep in mind that, as a general rule, short hair works best for shorter men. Long hair tends to hide the neck and shoulders, making your head and body look like one body part, which doesn't help you in your quest to look taller.

3. Another tip to maximize your stature is to stay fit and trim at all times. Heavier and extremely muscular men tend to look broader and stubbier, but staying lean and having some muscle (such as built, defined shoulders) can help add some height to your overall frame.

Whatever your body type, make sure your best features stand out while your less-than-perfect ones remain, for the most part, unnoticed. Don't try to overtly camouflage your weaker points; doing so will only accentuate them even more. The best way to illustrate this point is with the example of a balding man using a "comb-over" hairdo in an attempt to hide his bald spot; it only emphasizes the problem.

ARE YOU A FASHION VICTIM?

What exactly is a fashion victim? A fashion victim is someone who adopts trends slavishly, buying whatever the fashion authorities claim is stylish without taking other elements—such as his body type—into consideration. The end result is often an awkward, over-the-top style that makes him stick out like a sore thumb . . . not a good thing.

Too insecure in his own skin to decide what looks best on him, a fashion victim instead relies on the opinions of others when it comes to dressing himself. A fashion victim would be likely to purchase an expensive suit just because a slick salesman tells him "it's all the rage this season," without even paying attention to how the shoulders fit. He can't put himself together, whether his threads are worth $50 or $5,000, because his sole concern is looking hip. Yes, looking sharp does involve a certain degree of trendiness, but ultimately, your clothes have to fit right, and suit your style, image, and personality. **Remember, it's not about the clothes you wear—it's about how you wear them.**

HOW TO AVOID BEING A FASHION VICTIM

• *Be your own guide*

Wear what you think looks nice on you, not what others dictate is trendy. You should always feel comfortable with what you're wearing, so stick to items that suit your personality and regular style, all while keeping the occasion and setting in mind.

• *Less is more*

Don't overdo it. Even if your body type does lend itself to wearing trendy garments from head to toe, it's not a look you want to adopt. Buy several fashionable items every season, and mix and match them with the basics in your wardrobe. It's a smart (and cost-effective) way to look your best every day.

• *Don't be a sucker for brand names*

Try to avoid referring to your clothes by their designer labels (i.e., "my Boss belt" or "my Diesel Jeans"). By dissociating the item from its manufacturer, you will condition yourself to look at the item itself rather than be swayed by a brand name.

Before you decide to purchase a new item, ask yourself if you are buying it because it's "in style" or because it genuinely suits you. Ask yourself if you would buy the garment if it didn't have a logo on it.

SIGNS OF A GOOD FIT:
SHIRT, JACKET, AND PANTS

You can't determine if a garment fits you if you don't know how it's supposed to fit. The proper fits of your jacket, shirt, and pants are determined both relative to one another and relative to your body. So let's look at all three concurrently.

SHIRT COLLAR FIT #1
Your shirt collar should appear trim, but sit loose enough to accommodate comfort and future shrinkage (which is inevitable, whatever the salesman declares to the contrary). When you're trying a shirt on, a finger should fit between your neck and the collar with a bit of wriggle room to spare.

SHIRT COLLAR FIT #2
Half an inch of your shirt collar should be visible above your jacket collar.

JACKET COLLAR FIT
Your jacket collar should lie flat against the entire circumference of your shirt collar.

SHOULDER FIT
The shoulder line of your shirt and jacket should align with your body's natural shoulder line. The fit of your jacket here is especially important, if only because it is so visually apparent when it's off.

JACKET LENGTH
Your jacket should hang just long enough to cover your entire ass, but still afford your legs maximum length.

SLEEVE LENGTHS
When your arms are hanging loose at your side, your jacket's sleeve should extend to the first knuckle of thumb; where the wrist becomes the hand. Your shirt sleeve should extend a bit longer, so that half an inch of it is visible past the jacket cuff.

SHIRT CUFFS
The cuffs of your shirt should fit snugly but still accommodate comfortable movement. If you tuck your watch into your shirt cuff, it should stay there.

Note that this diagram addresses how garments should fall in their permanent, post-wash state. At point of purchase, depending on the fabric, you may want a garment to fall a bit looser to accommodate future shrinkage.

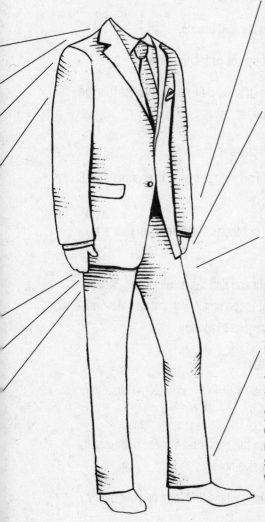

JACKET WAIST
When you button your jacket, it should cinch tightly enough around the waist to create slightly visible tension lines. If said tension lines extend into a large, pronounced X-shape, the jacket is too tight.

TROUSERS WAIST
The waist of dress trousers is designed to sit higher than casual pants. Nevertheless, you want them to sit comfortably, so wear them during your fitting as you anticipate doing regularly. This will ensure that your crotch is not dangling absurdly low in everyday use.

TROUSERS FIT
In keeping with the narrow silhouette that you've established from the waist up, your trousers should be trim throughout. Trim, but not tight—if your pants have pleats they should not be pulling open from tension.

TROUSERS BREAK
Your pants should break once on the top of your shoe, and only once. They should be cut slightly longer at the back, so they hang roughly an inch above the ground. We shouldn't see your socks when you're walking.

ENSURE A PROPER FIT

Neckties

The simplest way to ensure a well-fitted necktie is to have a well-fitted shirt to wear it with.

Here are some guidelines to remember:

- Your tie should hang just above your belt buckle.

- The tie knot should not force the tips of your shirt collar up.

- The inverted triangle of the tie knot should fit neatly into the triangle created by your buttoned-up shirt collar.

Overcoats

- Buy a coat that's one size larger than your suit size, to ensure that it'll fit over your sweaters and suits.

- The coat's sleeve should rest at your thumb knuckle when your arm is hanging loose at your side.

- The coat's back should lie straight and flat, like a suit jacket. Horizontal wrinkles are a sign that the coat is too small. Vertical wrinkles indicate that the coat is too large, and requires tailoring.

Belts

- When it comes to belts, you should buy one size bigger than your pants. A 34" waist requires a 36" belt.

- The buckle's notch should fit into the center hole of the belt (usually hole number three; most belts have five holes).

- The tail of the belt should end just past the first loop on your pants.

- The edge of the belt buckle, the row of buttons on your shirt, and your fly should all line up vertically.

HOW TO HIDE FLAWS WITH CLOTHING

There are general rules of thumb that apply to generic body types. However, few of us guys have bodies that fall perfectly into some body-type template— and oftentimes, our imperfections are what distinguish our frames.

So how do you dress well if you've got a gut? How do you disguise a short waist? What exactly is the procedure for camouflaging a flat butt? And what kind of jeans should you wear if you've got a big butt?

Thankfully, there are solutions. Welcome to the world of "clothes as body camouflage," where anything is possible.

Short-waisted

Simply put, short-waistedness is when your legs are longer than your torso. It's almost always a product of genetics, but it shouldn't prove to be any trouble for you if you follow these simple tips when dressing casual.

- Wear jeans or slacks at your hips, not at your waist.

- Don't tuck in; wear pullovers instead of button-downs to disguise your waist/hips.

- Wear tall-cut T-shirts.

- Match the color of your top with your belt. This will give the illusion that your torso is longer.

- Wear sweaters and jackets that hang below your waist.

- For the short-waisted man, pulling off suits is trickier than casual clothes. For starters, you should match the color tones of your jacket, pants, and dress shirt to create one seamless outfit, or look. In other words, don't throw on a pink shirt with a black suit if you're short-waisted, as it provides too much of a contrast.

- Cuffed legs will make your lower half seem shorter.

Long-waisted

If you're long-waisted, your legs are relatively short and your torso is long. There are several ways to address this with some simple clothing adjustments.

■ Wear a T-shirt, sweater, or shirt in a contrasting color to your pants. This will break up the vertical line of your body.

■ Do the opposite of the short-waisted man and wear your pants at the waist, not at the hips.

■ Tuck in your shirts.

■ Wearing suspenders will also create the illusion of a higher waistline.

■ A belt with a large buckle and pleated, uncuffed slacks will draw attention to your lower half and make your legs appear longer.

Flat butt

A flat butt can cause pants to drape awkwardly and shirts to simply fall off into the air.

You can begin overcoming a flat ass by staying away from baggy clothes. Billowy pants will make your lower half look as if it's trapped in a parachute. Instead of thinking "bigger is better," wear jeans or pants that are fitted around the waist and include a high inseam. This cut supports the butt you *do* have, and makes it a shade more prominent. Straight-legged pants will also draw attention away from your backside by keeping the lower part of your legs in proportion with your hips, waist, and butt.

Big butt

A big butt is not necessarily bad news. Most women even prefer guys who have a toned "bubble butt." Still, if you want to trim your caboose, try boxer briefs or biking shorts as an undergarment. These will help pull your butt and upper thighs tightly up.

If your butt sticks out at the top (kind of like a ledge), check out looser, wider-fitting jeans with a boot cut (we'll explore the various kinds of denim cuts in a later chapter). These cuts provide a smoother vertical line when paired with pullovers and T-shirts.

For the truly bottom-heavy, avoid pleated trousers, which can highlight your hips; flat-front pants are more slimming when it comes to your thighs and trunk. Top off your look with a three quarter–length jacket, and that big butt will quickly become just another part of your body.

Big belly

How to camouflage a big belly is the kind of knowledge almost every guy needs at some point in his life.

- *Opt for light fabrics, dark colors*

Start by avoiding tweed, flannel, and other heavy fabrics. Go with light, natural fabrics, and dress in dark, muted colors.

- *Wear undergarments*

For business casual wear, opt for an undershirt and tuck it in. Then throw on a pullover or sweater. The undershirt keeps your belly in place, while the pullover creates that all-important (and quite slimming) vertical line for your figure (provided your pants fit nicely).

- *Avoid T-shirts in general*

Baggy T-shirts only make you look bigger, and tight T-shirts emphasize your gut. Stick with long sleeves; they'll make your body look more proportional and "together."

Underdeveloped chest

Let's face it: Droopy pectorals, a sunken chest and small, rounded shoulders can all do a number on how others view you, and how you view yourself.

To turn your small chest into an inverted triangle fit for a superhero, start wearing colored shirts, jackets, and ties, preferably with horizontal stripes. While dark colors and vertical stripes slim the body, colors and horizontal stripes expand it.

The colored garments on your upper body will look all the more striking if you contrast them with darker-colored pants. Be warned, however: If you choose colors that are too light, people are liable to see right through your shirt and get a glimpse of your chest.

You can also "expand" your chest by wearing heavier fabrics. Stay away from the silks and nylons of the world, and instead stock up on heavy cottons, tweeds, flannels, and thick-knit sweaters (during the colder months, of course).

Embrace layers. Make an undershirt, a button-down shirt, a sweater, and a jacket/coat your standard cool weather outfit.

When it comes to suits, opt for shoulder pads and a double-breasted cut. The latter will expand your mid-section and create a boxier, larger look. If the double-breasted look doesn't suit your style palate, a single-breasted suit with wide lapels and double vents should do the job.

Long or skinny arms

If you possess long, underdeveloped arms, you can embrace many of the tenets outlined for the chap with the underdeveloped chest. Begin by wearing long sleeves in thick fabrics and in layers.

In hot weather, try to draw attention to your neckline. V-neck T-shirts and ringer tees will draw eyes away from your arms and to your upper chest.

Be sure, however, that the sleeves extend to within a couple inches of your elbows. Short-sleeve tees will put you in the unenviable position of emphasizing muscles you don't possess.

If you have long arms but some muscle definition, fret not; retailers know you're out there. Plenty of retail outlets stock broad lines of "tall cut" shirts that guarantee the long-limbed man never need worry about exposed wrists.

Long, skinny neck

A long, skinny neck can make your upper body look gangly, with sharp corners and defined bones. To eliminate this look, wear well-starched, long-sleeve shirts with widely spread collars. The collar's openness will make a thin neck appear thicker by giving a hint of the upper shoulders, as well as creating a wider shoulder line.

A wider tie knot with a horizontal pattern will also help create the illusion of a fuller neck.

When donning more casual attire, both turtlenecks and crew necks are solid choices. Conversely, you should avoid V-neck sweaters and V-neck tees, as their downward-oriented cut will only serve to make your neck appear longer and skinnier.

Short, fat neck or double chin

Remember, V-neck pullovers and tees help draw the eye downward, making your neckline lower and your neck appear longer. A regular point collar on your more formal shirts and a tie with vertical stripes will also visually lengthen it.

Buy jackets with thin lapels. Wide lapels emphasize width— something you don't need to do.

Flattering fashion

Don't let clothing camouflage be your only recourse to overcoming body flaws. A nice pair of shoes, eye-pleasing accessories, good hair, and a clear complexion will all help in the quest to move observers' eyes away from the parts of your body you'd rather not advertise.

RULE 2
COLLECT YOUR STAPLES

The process of learning which clothes suit you personally might seem to be a limiting one, in that it confines potential purchases to your particular mold. The end result of this process, however, typically proves to be the opposite. Your style eye, suddenly more refined and sophisticated, will no longer scan retail racks indiscriminately, waiting for the something that you "like" to randomly fall under your gaze. You are now armed with criteria, and you will rapidly come to the potentially expensive discovery that a lot of clothing out there meets it.

Resisting splurging on a stock of clothes simply because they suit you isn't just an economical measure. It's part of your second strategy—and our second rule—in populating your wardrobe. Having established what clothes fit you individually, let's now take a look at the garments that have historically found a place in all male wardrobes, and will continue to do so throughout the remainder of your lifespan.

CLASSIC PIECES EVERY MAN SHOULD OWN

The backbone of a stylish male wardrobe requires certain essential, well-crafted pieces. Because these items are enduringly chic, they should be of sufficiently good quality to last for multiple seasons. Some may require a significant initial investment, but their long lifespan will often warrant the investment.

These items are the wardrobe and accessory staples every man should own; the things so ingrained into our lives that even after one of them falls apart, we go out and buy another in the very same style. Just be sure to follow the golden rule of selecting staple items when shopping: Stick to neutral colors such as black, brown, gray, navy, white, and tan as they can be easily matched with each other or brighter colors if need be. With that rule in mind, read on to discover which pieces will help you to achieve your smoothest style ever.

Black dress shirt

Bold and confident, a black dress shirt looks striking whether paired with jeans or dress pants. The only rule to remember: Don't wear this piece with a black suit . . . unless you're attending a funeral.

What you can wear it with: Jeans, dress pants, and accessories.

Overcoat

Of obvious worth during cold weather, an overcoat can also spruce up your professional image. But sticking with single-breasted styles, subtle colors and popular fabrics like cashmere can net you an overcoat that will last for years.

What you can wear it with: Overcoats can look killer with a blazer, though in cold weather they look good with just about anything.

Scarf

Tie a scarf around your neck and you'll seem like you've mastered the art of being effortlessly cool. Choose one made of quality fabric such as cashmere, wool, or a silk blend for durability.

What you can wear it with: You can wear scarves with nearly anything, from just a sweater on an early fall afternoon, to your thickest overcoat in winter months. Just be sure that the quality of your scarf is equivalent or superior to that of the outerwear you pair it with.

Brown dress shoes

For a truly versatile wardrobe, brown dress shoes are as important as black ones.

What you can wear them with: Beige or navy blue trousers show them off to their best advantage, and they can be worn with anything except black bottoms.

Cashmere sweater

Supremely luxurious, cashmere is as soft and comfortable as it is refined. No well-dressed man's wardrobe should be without a sweater made of this fine fabric. Although it's expensive, good-quality cashmere will last forever when cared for properly. Look for two-ply cashmere, as it will resist holes, and choose grade-A cashmere for a sweater that is less likely to pill (accumulate balls of fuzz on its surface).

What you can wear it with: A fine sweater will pair well with either jeans or slacks and your favorite blazer.

Leather belt

A leather belt with a silver buckle is an absolute necessity in any man's wardrobe, and fortunately, good-quality belts can be had at reasonable prices. Belts are sort of like referees and waiters; they're at their best when you don't notice them that much. The key to a classic belt is to avoid anything that disrupts its slight concealment among clothes, meaning anything that jumps out, like large ostentatious buckles or shiny, flashy leather. To get the most bang for your buck, go for one that is reversible, with black on one side and brown on the other.

What you can wear it with: Jeans, flat-front pants, and suits.

White T-shirt

For a fresh and wholesome all-American look, you can't beat the white T-shirt and jeans combo. You need not limit yourself to jeans with this T-shirt, however, as it can be paired with anything you might also wear with a dress shirt to give it a more casual-cool effect. Look for a blend of 98% cotton and 2% Lycra as the stretch from the Lycra means the shirt will fit you to a T, in addition to ensuring the garment retains its shape over time.

What you can wear it with: Provided you avoid overly large sizes, you can wear your trusty white T-shirt with jeans or shorts when it's warm, or as an undergarment under sweaters and shirts in the winter.

White dress shirt

The ultimate timeless piece. Think of this classic as a crisp, clean white canvas on which to showcase other trendier items of your wardrobe. No matter what you wear with it, you'll look instantly put together and a decent one won't cost you the Earth. Pay attention to details, though, and choose a thicker cotton weave for increased durability.

What you can wear it with: What *can't* you wear this with? Ideal for both suits and jeans of all colors, the white shirt is truly your closet's most valuable player.

Sports coat

Every man knows that, like the white shirt, a good solid-color jacket can be used in numerous situations and can often make shabby-looking ensembles respectable. Obviously, the simpler the sports coat, the more enduring its timelessness; fabrics like corduroy, and anything with pinstripes, are more high risk.

What you can wear it with: Your sports coat can be worn at the office with a matching pair of suit pants, or in a bar with a pair of your most reliable blue jeans.

Black socks

Unless you're playing sports or hanging out in your pajamas, stay away from white socks. Instead, choose black socks both for everyday wear and for special occasions. To ensure your socks go with all of your clothes, pick black socks that are smooth (no ribbing) and fairly thin with reinforced toes. Since socks are fairly cheap and wear out quickly, make sure you buy a few new sets every six months.

What you can wear them with: Anything but your gym shoes.

A suit

While the classic, staple suit certainly merits a place on this list, it also deserves far more exploration than the present space permits. So for the time being just add it to your list; we'll take you through all the ins and outs in a later chapter.

Black dress shoes

They say your shoes get noticed first, so make sure you invest in a good pair. A modern, sleek take on the classic cap-toe oxford is your best bet for a black dress shoe you can wear with anything. Pass on clunky dress shoes or those with heels greater than one-quarter to one-half of an inch, as these will be difficult to wear with a slim-cut suit.

What you can wear them with: Suits and formal attire.

Polo shirt

Typically a short-sleeved, collared shirt made from cotton, polo shirts are the definition of classy, coolly assured casual dress. No matter what your age, a polo shirt will always look fetching. Loads of companies, like Lacoste and Ralph Lauren, make polos in a variety of colors and patterns, so get a few different shirts if you want to give a trendy twist to this must-have item.

What you can wear it with: Khakis, jeans, or slacks.

Jeans

There probably isn't a North American man alive that does not own at least one pair of blue jeans. From Levi's to Diesel, the original blue jeans can be slightly faded or a dirty denim, and yet they're still so programmed in our society that we continue to buy them, regardless of trends.

You don't have to break the bank buying these, but you do need to be certain they fit properly, meaning they showcase what's great about your body. They should also be seriously comfortable since you'll be wearing them a lot. Look for a comfortably soft denim weave, but make sure the fabric is thick enough to withstand daily wear and tear.

What you can wear them with: Versatility is the name of the game here, and rightly so, as blue jeans look good with nearly anything, from a blazer and dress shoes to a T-shirt and sneakers.

COMPLETING THE LOOK: ESSENTIAL ACCESSORIES

Sunglasses

Not only useful on the beach, every man should have a pair in his car. To make a strong impression in the style department, look for something timeless. Avoid big, clunky models. Black frames and dark lenses are typically universally flattering and will complement any outfit.

What you can wear them with: Because of their practicality on sunny days, you can wear sunglasses with just about anything, summer or winter.

Black leather wallet

Considering how important wallets are to guys, you should get one that will never go out of style. Stay away from anything with Velcro or slogans on it.

What you can wear it with: Anything, just as long as you don't leave home without it.

Steel-band watch

A steel-banded watch will never let you down for a casual or sporty style. Many are also waterproof, so this type of watch is a great choice for active individuals. To ensure your watch goes with all your weekend gear, keep it simple when selecting the face design and avoid straps that are too bulky or extremely thin. Round shapes, subtle numbering and colors (think silver, black, or gray), and steel straps are stylish enough to look great, but restrained and traditional enough to buck the trends. Lastly, stay away from gadgets and gizmos like GPS, as they cheapen the look of any watch.

What you can wear it with: Like most daily accessories, your watch should look and feel good with everything you wear.

Leather-band watch

Black and brown leather-band watches are the best choices when selecting a watch for versatility. As well, check to see how durable the leather is when purchasing this type of watch because a strap that's too thin might break within the first year of use. With a leather strap, a watch face that is square and steel looks best and is never out of style.

What you can wear it with: Both everyday and formal attire.

Leather gloves

Any impeccable wardrobe should include a pair of gloves that, well, fit like a glove. If cold weather is an issue, cashmere-lined gloves will solve that problem. Gloves with ruching on the inside of the wrist will also help prevent cold air from damaging your digits.

What you can wear it with: Similar to a watch or sunglasses, these are a daily cold-season accessory, and will pair well with anything you wear.

Cologne/Aftershave

For most men, cologne and aftershave application is such a daily routine that a particular scent becomes part of their identity. For something that won't fall out of fashion, stay away from strongly scented colognes.

What you can wear it with: Everything from a bathrobe to a business suit.

Umbrella

Every man should own at least one umbrella, if not more, ideally with one always in the trunk of the car. While the umbrella's worth may be more practical than aesthetic, if you want to ensure longevity, you should stick to solid, dark colors and avoid patterns and designs. Also, the shorter, more compact styles might be easier to transport, but for sheer traditional looks, long, sleek models are the way to go.

What you can wear it with: A two-piece suit and an overcoat, but good for any occasion, especially while getting caught in the rain with a date.

CLOTHING TO INVEST IN

It would be nice if assembling a wardrobe depended solely upon taste and adherence to the staples, but for most of us, finances are also a governing factor. When budgeting for clothes, you want to invest in the staples that merit it, but you also want to pay more for what people will notice and less for what they won't. There's no point, for example, on spending $200 on a pair of socks that no one will see. Splurge on a quality suit, however, and you'll cut a dashing figure at any event.

Confused about which pieces to drop your hard-earned cash on and when to save your money? Read on to find out which items are worth a little extra investment and how you can save on the stuff no one will notice.

Cuff links

They may be small, but cuff links speak volumes about your sense of style. It's the little details that count the most and few other accessories can add so much instant class and polish to your look.

Expect to pay: $100 to $300

Watch

A great watch will last you the rest of your life and will stylishly enhance anything you wear. Make sure you buy a timeless piece; go for something with a black leather band and a silver face.

Expect to pay: $500 to . . . the sky's the limit

Overcoat

You wear it every day for much of the year and it's what people initially see on you, so consider what kind of first impression you want to make when you buy your overcoat. You probably won't own too many coats, so make the one you do own an invaluable addition to your wardrobe. A great coat will complement your work clothes handsomely and will even add style to a jeans-and-T-shirt look.

Expect to pay: $500 to $1,500

Suit

Invest in one good, classic-cut suit and you'll live in it for the next ten years. Many guys hesitate to splurge on suits because they anticipate wearing them only a few times each year; what they don't realize is that the more flattering a suit is, the more occasions you'll find to employ it. We'll look at suits in detail in Chapter 8.

Expect to pay: $1,000 to $2,500

Sunglasses

This is the accessory that will make you look cool all year round, conceal hangovers, and get you noticed right away. Black or darkly tinted lenses are most alluring and will never go out of style; stay away from flashy-colored lenses or frames.

Expect to pay: $150 to $600

CLOTHING TO SAVE ON

Casual shirts

Never spend more than necessary on basics like T-shirts and casual dress shirts. These pieces will be worn and washed often, and will therefore wear out more quickly. Changing up your shirts every so often is also a very inexpensive and easy way to keep up with trends and ensure that your look stays fresh.

Expect to pay: No more than $30 for T-shirts, and no more than $50 for casual dress shirts

Socks and underwear

As long as you stick with solid black socks, you can save money on them because, quite frankly, no one will notice. Great-looking underwear can also be purchased inexpensively. Check out sales in department stores for discounts on designer duds. In lower-end department stores you can also buy underwear cheaply; just stick with standard patterns or solid colors and avoid no-name designer logos and weird pictures (like Papa Smurf, which will terrify first-time bed partners).

Expect to pay: $10 for a pack of three or for one designer pair on sale

Ties

Save on ties, but take into account the texture of the tie and be sure to choose only ties made from quality materials—such as silk—as these feel much nicer to wear (and be tied up in).

Expect to pay: $20 to $30

Belts

A truly useful item, the solid black, leather belt with a silver buckle shouldn't cost you much and you'll wear it for years before it falls apart.

Expect to pay: $30 to $60

TIPS FOR BUYING COLLARED SHIRTS

The white collared shirt is man's answer to the woman's little black dress; a style canvas with almost limitless matching possibilities. Its timeless value resides in its versatility, and its versatility arises from its simplicity, but it is this very simplicity that prompts so many of us to be excessively casual in purchasing it. Too many guys buy collared shirts the same way they buy socks or underwear: as items that require little consideration, because they're only going to be worn *under* something.

Well, that's the attitude of the man who doesn't know how to flatter himself with a collared shirt, one that you're about to shed. In Rule 1 we showed you how to fit a shirt, now let's look at how to determine if a shirt fits its price tag.

Signs of a Good Shirt

As a man grows progressively better versed in sartorial matters, he rapidly comes to the realization that much of the advice offered in clothing stores is gobbledygook. Emerging from a retail outlet without getting hustled is a matter of self-reliance; you simply cannot trust an anonymous salesman to give you an honest account of a garment's quality relative to its price. That's why you will memorize the chart that follows, and silently reference it the next time a clerk dangles an outrageously priced shirt under your nose.

These signs of quality are not set out here as necessary ingredients for every shirt purchase—if you demand that every shirt demonstrate all of them, you will blaze through your clothing budget pretty quickly. We present them simply as reference points to help you distill fact from fiction the next time you're faced with a pushy salesman.

FIRM COLLAR:

Better collars are firm, crisp, and smooth. If you see wrinkling in a collar that hasn't even left the rack, take it as an indication of future deterioration.

COLLAR TABS:

These small pieces of plastic or metal are inserted into the underside of the collar points to maintain their stiffness. Good shirts have them; poorer-quality shirts don't.

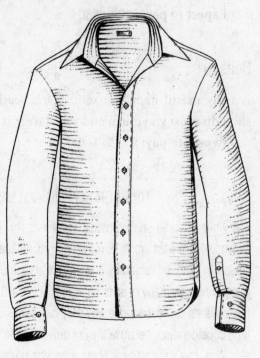

THREAD COUNT:

The higher, the better. Premium shirts can exceed 200 threads per inch, but there's no need to go crazy here. Any count above 140 will put you into pretty nice territory.

SINGLE-STITCH SEAMS:

In most shirts that you'll encounter, two rows of stitching will be visible in the side seam. Rarer are those that exhibit only a single line, a sound hallmark of quality.

ALIGNED PATTERNS:

In a high-grade shirt, patterns are aligned on either side of a seam, so as to create the illusion of a single, flowing piece of fabric.

SPLIT YOKE:

Also known as a two-piece yoke. The yoke is the panel of the shirt that spans the upper back; a split in it accommodates the prospect of detailed alterations, and is typically reserved for those who can afford such alterations (or to promote the illusion of such).

WORKING SLEEVE PLACKET BUTTONS:
The sleeve placket is the vent above the cuffs. A working button here is one marker of quality; a horizontal buttonhole to accommodate it, rather than a vertical one, is an indication that you're dealing with some premium stuff.

COLLAR STYLES

Collar flaps are known as points. The space between the points is known as the spread. From here, categorizing shirt collars gets a little more complex—but nothing that you can't handle.

There are a wide variety of collars to choose from, and those who wish to dedicate the research can explore such collars as the Johnny Collar, the Peter Pan Collar, the Medici Collar, and the Cossack Collar. For present purposes, however, we'll focus on the Big 6:

Wing Collar

The points of the collar stand up and then flatten out horizontally. Its use is typically restricted to evening formal wear. (Barristers in the UK, however, wear them to work.)

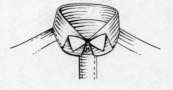

Button-Down Collar

A visible button holds each point in place. Popularized by Brooks Brothers, and today associated with Vermont college professors and television home repair personalities.

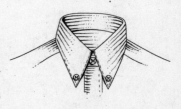

Pin Collar

A hole in each collar allows for the insertion of a metal bar (usually a gold one) that

spans the spread and keeps the points in place. Stylish in the minds of some, but ostentatious in those of others. Think of the pin collar as a French cuff for the neck.

Tab Collar

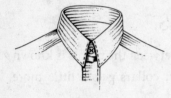

A fabric band spanning the spread holds each point in place. This band is designed to be concealed by the tie knot that rests on top of it. Not to be confused with the collar tab (or collar stay), the small piece of plastic or metal is inserted into the underside of the points to maintain their stiffness.

Club Collar

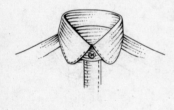

The points of the collar are not pointed at all, but in fact small and rounded. Also known as the Eton Collar, the Club Collar is usually associated with turn-of-the-century schoolboys or strange and troubled older men.

Turn-Down Collar

The regular collar you are most familiar with. Simple though it may appear, the Turn-Down Collar gives rise to a host of variations, based on both the length of the point (which can be classified as either short, medium or long) and, more importantly, the width of the spread. A very widely spread collar is known as a *cutaway*; a smaller spread one is said to have *straight points*.

Determining the right collar to wear depends upon two factors:

1. The size of your tie knot: Your collar should frame your tie knot. So the wider the knot, the wider a spread you'll need to accommodate it. For example, one might look to a cutaway to pair with the bulky Windsor knot (see Master Different Tie Knots, pages 96–102), whereas a narrower spread lends itself to the narrower Four-In-Hand knot.

2. The shape of your face and neck: One simple rule of thumb here is that short necks require short collars, and long necks require long ones. While this is the clearest principle regarding face/collar-matching, it is unfortunately not the only one. Most of the remainder, however, can be neatly summarized in Alan Flusser's quote:

> *"Think of your face as a portrait and your shirt collar as its frame."*

The author of *The Suit: A Machiavellian Approach to Men's Style* expands further upon this notion:

> *"Just as it would be unreasonable to cram* The Night Watch *into a frame made for* Self Portrait in a Cap, *so do wide faces look like bowling balls atop small collars, narrow faces like golf balls on big collars; and long necks look stork-like in low collars, and short necks disappear in high collars."*

SIZING UP A COLLAR

Choosing the shirt's collar is an important step in the selection process. Your collar should sit evenly on your neck, without choking you. As a rule of thumb, you should be able to slip in a finger comfortably. Take future shrinkage into account when trying on a shirt pre-purchase.

WHICH SHIRTS TO BUY FIRST

You've been given guidance on how to gauge the quality of a dress shirt. So now that you're prepared to make the investment, here is the order in which you should do so.

1. White button-cuff turndown collar

The outstanding value of this garment lies in its versatility—it's no exaggeration to declare that the simple white dress shirt can be matched with any formal wear. For this very reason (coupled with the fact that they make the ideal canvas for dirt), your white shirts will wear out quickly, and you'll find that you never have enough of them.

2. White button-cuff turndown collar

That's how integral the simple white shirt is: it takes the top two slots on this list. But don't mistake your extended supply as a cue to extend their use into your casual wardrobe. Dress shirts tend to be cut longer so as to prevent inadvertent untucking, and many are cut of near-translucent cloth. So wearing them with jeans will make you look ridiculous. If you want to wear casual white shirts casually, you'll need to stock up on button-downs designed for casual wear.

3. Light blue button-cuff turndown collar

Move into bolder territory with baby steps. You'll go blue to add some variety to your formal wardrobe, but light blue to preserve your versatility (dark blue being particularly difficult to match).

4. White French cuff turndown collar

French cuffs are made for use with cuff links; they cannot be worn without cuff links. Because you want to preserve the power and visual impact of your cuff links, you'll wait for the most top-shelf occasions to bust this combo out. But because said occasions can sneak up on you, you'll have a white French cuff hanging on your fourth hanger in preparation.

5. Patterned button-cuff turndown collar

We won't go into further detail as regards type of pattern than to suggest that you keep things simple. Your first patterned shirt should be set against a white or light blue background and adhere to regular spacing.

As with all matters of style, with practice, your boldness in selecting shirts will increase, as will your confidence in this matter. Just be sure to never lose sight of the basics, and always keep some fresh whites in the purchase rotation.

A GUIDE TO OVERCOATS

By definition, an overcoat is a heavy coat worn over ordinary clothing—from suits to more casual attire—in cold weather. Overcoats join suits and dress shoes in the "garments to buy for life" category. Accordingly, they merit a bit of additional investment and plenty of additional consideration in advance of their purchase.

You want an overcoat that will:

1. Suit your body type

2. Look as stylish in 2050 as it did in 1950

This may seem daunting on the surface, but it's simply a matter of sticking to the classics; those overcoats that have endured and will likely continue to do so. With that in mind, and recalling the subject of our first chapter, you'll be able to hone in on the time-tested styles that suit your body type.

4 CLASSIC OVERCOATS

Pea coat

Also known as a reefer jacket or pilot jacket, the pea coat first found favor among the European navies of the 18th century. The U.S. Navy jumped on the bandwagon in the early 20th century, giving us the double-breasted, wool variation that persists today.

A classic since: At least 1717, the year that the *Oxford English Dictionary* first references the use of the term.

Three quarter–length dress coat

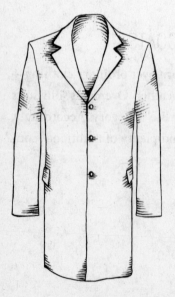

Frustratingly, there is no single universal term for this most classic of overcoats. It is casually referred to as an overcoat. When more precision is demanded, varying descriptive terms are used: full-length, knee-length, etc. Go for the classic, single-breasted, three- or four-button variety, preferably in a navy or midnight blue.

A classic since: The mid-18th century, in the variation illustrated here.

Duffle coat

The Duffle coat is most recognizable for its wooden toggle fasteners, which lend it something of a childish character. These buttons weren't created for fat little kiddie fingers, however; they were designed for the frosty, gloved fingers of British navy seamen. Ditto for the hood, which is oversized to accommodate a naval cap. The term "duffle" derives from the Belgian town that produces the wool traditionally used in manufacturing these coats.

A classic since: 1890, when the Englishman John Partridge first coupled the fabric with his overcoat design.

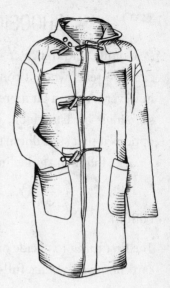

Trench coat

Two trench coats exist in the popular consciousness: the ominous black trench coat worn by killers and Scandinavian death metal guitarists, and the tan, belted raincoat. When we close our eyes and picture the latter, we will either see it on an unstylish salesman or a rather stylish young man, depending on the era in which we live. Like the aviator sunglasses, tan trench coats move in and out of fashion currency. But also like the aviators, they have sustained this cycle for so long that we can lend them classic status.

A classic since: 1901, when the coat's designer, Thomas Burberry, successfully pitched it to the UK War Office as an addition to the service uniform.

CHOOSING A DRESS OVERCOAT

Pea, duffle, and trench coats all offer little in the way of variation, which can be a relief when it comes time to choose one. Selecting a dress coat, however, can be a bit more challenging. And while we advocate the classic, single-breasted look, you shouldn't shy away from exploring your options if that style doesn't strike you as a suitable one.

The following guidelines will help you narrow down your search.

Length

The first thing to decide on when purchasing an overcoat is length. You can choose between a full-length or a three quarter–length overcoat.

Full-length

A full-length overcoat usually looks dressier than a three quarter–length one. They also seem to be more popular amongst older men. Longer overcoats tend to suit taller men more favorably than their shorter counterparts, as longer overcoats may make "vertically challenged" guys look stockier and shorter than they really are.

A full-length jacket should fall around the lower level of your shins, which is perfect for those colder winter days. On the flip side, the lower part of the jacket might get dirtier once the snow starts to melt.

Three quarter–length

A three quarter–length overcoat should fall anywhere between the lower part of your knee and the lower part of your trousers' pockets. This is definitely a younger, more fashionable choice. A well-tailored three quarter–length overcoat is also sure to mold your body perfectly.

Single or double-breasted?

Single-breasted

A single-breasted overcoat closes with a narrow overlap and fastens down in front with a single row of buttons. You'll usually find three- or four-button single-breasted overcoats.

A single-breasted overcoat is generally more practical, as it can be worn open and doesn't always need to be buttoned up. A well-tailored single-breasted overcoat also provides a more slimming appearance.

Double-breasted

To fasten a double-breasted overcoat, you'll have to lap one edge of the front well over the other. It usually presents a double row of buttons with a single row of buttonholes.

Double-breasted overcoats will go in and out of style every few years, which is another reason to advocate the single-breasted look.

Fit

Make sure your overcoat fits squarely around your shoulders and waist (try it on over a suit). Obvious shoulder pads are definitely out of style, so all you wannabe football stars, please restrain yourselves.

Details

You can always find great looking overcoats that provide retractable lining. Zip on the lining in colder weather, and simply zip it off once the temperature warms up.

You should also look out for pockets, which are always practical whether they're at the waist, hip, or chest level.

JACKETS VS. BLAZERS

While the blazer has its roots firmly planted in sport jacket history, subtle style differences make the two wardrobe pieces very distinct from one another. The difference between them is often misunderstood, and this confusion likely stems from the fact that neither a jacket nor a blazer has a matching pair of pants. Despite this similarity, however, there do exist major differences, the foremost being that a sport jacket is textured and oftentimes patterned, whereas a blazer is a solid, dark color (usually navy or black), made of smooth fabric, and usually seen with naval-style brass buttons.

To avoid confusing the two styles any further, learn more about the differences between a jacket and a blazer; this way you'll avert any unbecoming fashion blunders.

Sport jacket

The sport jacket derives from the experimentation with sports clothes in the mid-19th century. By the early 20th century, men were seeking comfort and high fashion in their clothing, and turned to the ever-evolving sport jacket as a fashion-forward, casual answer to laidback social functions—meaning, an afternoon at a stuffy gentleman's club or sitting on the sidelines of a tennis match. The male leisure landscape may have changed since then, but its casual use remains intact.

Odd jacket

Named after its lack of matching trousers, the odd jacket was known mostly as sporting-event and clubhouse attire. The odd jacket is also known for incorporating distinctive detailing like pleats, stitched belts, and offbeat pockets into the ever-evolving design. The blazer is often described as a derivative of the odd jacket, although it incorporates enough differences to belong in a category all its own.

Patterned sport jacket

The patterned sport jacket appeared after World War II to accommodate the business-casual lifestyle men began to adopt. Incorporating bold patterns like Shetland stripes (seen on Ivy League campuses) and madras plaids (seen in colleges and country clubs), patterned sport jackets were a way for the fashion-conscious modern man to avoid having his jacket embarrassingly mistaken for a suit jacket.

Blazer

By 1938, blazers were the fashionable odd jacket of choice for style connoisseurs. With its origins in the English cricket club scene, the blazer was often striped and in club colors. This look eventually evolved to include brass buttons, single and double-breasted models, and a club badge on the breast pocket. Blazers are offered in a variety of styles with different detail options, including flap or patch pockets, and peak or notch lapels. Depending on your blazer style of choice and what you pair it with, blazers are easier to dress down than sport jackets.

Nautical blazer

Navy-colored blazers adorned with brass buttons were predominant throughout the 1920s, and made a stylish sport outfit when paired with white pants. And due to their lightweight fabric, these nautical-inspired blazers were summer fashion sensations.

Colored blazer

Blazers rightfully got their name because they were "blazed" with more color and bolder patterns than the refined sport jacket. Blazers weren't only striped, but they also came in a variety of bright colors, like powder blue and purple, and they made their way into men's weekend-wear wardrobes.

Modern-day dos and don'ts

■ The bold patterns and heavy tweed fabric of the sport jacket make it inappropriate for business or formal wear. Pair it with denim or corduroy for more casual outings.

■ If you're going to wear a blazer, keep the breast pocket bare; don't adorn it with a badge unless you wear your blazer for club purposes.

■ Nowadays, traditional double-breasted, brass-buttoned nautical blazers are usually worn by older men (we're talking the grandpa generation here). In other words: Don't do it.

■ Single-breasted blazers, whether navy or colored *without* the brass buttons, are modern and versatile as they can be dressed up with flannel trousers or dressed down with denim. And they can be accessorized with the most formal of ascots or the most basic of ties.

■ Your only choice when attending a formal event, such as a business meeting or a wedding, is to disregard both the jacket and the blazer and wear a suit.

Although often confused, the sport jacket and the blazer are two very different items of clothing. They each have their respective places in history, and each has its own distinctive method of being worn. So while they might both be jacket-like, sport jackets and blazers certainly aren't cut from the same cloth.

RULE 3
SHOES MAKE THE MAN

Shoes are and forever will be the most important fashion item that you buy. People will look at them and judge you by them, and if they don't approve of them, the effect of the rest of your ensemble—the gorgeous watch and perfectly cut suit—will be entirely negated.

This is frustrating to many men, because shoes are expensive and a true pain in the ass to shop for. To those men we say, stop your bleating already. If you're smart about buying shoes, you won't have to buy again for years, if not decades. Furthermore, the returns on your investment are immediate—quality shoes are an instant confidence booster. The smack of a heavy sole against pavement is a very satisfying sound when you're the one producing it: it rings of authority and calls attention to your investment (and with it, your standing as a man of style).

If you still have doubts as to the importance of shoes, turn to a woman. Don't ask her for her opinion; simply wear your finest pair and wait for her to notice and praise them. After she does, you will never scrimp on shoes again.

HOW MUCH SHOULD I SPEND ON SHOES?

Good shoes are expensive. On the high end of the scale, they can cost you almost as much as a decent suit or watch (approaching the four-digit range). On the lower end, they will fetch at least $250 to $300. This is really the minimum amount that you should be spending.

If those numbers make you cringe, they shouldn't. A good pair of shoes truly is an investment that will last you for a long time. You may have to replace the soles every once in a while, but it's not unheard of for a man's shoes to last him twenty, or even thirty years.

Of course, sustaining that lifespan demands maintenance. And if you're going to actually wear a pair over that extended a period, they'll have to be timeless in their style. Succumbing to fleeting trends in purchasing expensive shoes is best left to the outrageously wealthy.

We'll instruct you on both maintenance and shoes styles later in this chapter. But first, let's address our primary criterion: finding shoes that fit *you*.

HOW TO GET THE BEST FIT

Good fit is the most important factor to consider when purchasing new footwear. There's no point in buying shoes that will pinch your toes and cramp your feet all day long. Sporting uncomfortable shoes for long periods of time isn't only unbearable, but could also permanently damage your feet and your overall posture. Make that extra effort to find a pair of shoes that feel great on your feet.

Shopping for comfort

When shopping for shoes, always remember to bring along your own pair of socks. Bring the kind of socks that you plan on wearing with your prospective purchase; if you're going to be wearing thin silk socks with your new oxfords, there's little point in trying them on with thick athletic socks.

Shoe stores normally have spare pairs of socks hanging around if ever you need them, but a slight difference in thickness could affect the fit substantially.

Once you've slipped on both shoes, lace or buckle them up the way you normally would and take your time in walking around the store. You should feel at ease and comfortable during your entire tryout. Your shoes should be snug enough to hold your feet firmly while still allowing enough room to wiggle your toes.

Your feet tend to slightly swell up over the course of the day, because of the hours of walking and standing that they endure. As a result, you should try on shoes at the end of the day in order to ensure that they will be comfortable throughout.

Remember: you're the customer. So if a salesperson tries to pressure you into buying by telling you that the shoe will stretch if they feel too tight, for example, politely tell him to take a walk of his own. Don't assume that with time your shoes will stretch out and feel better—your feet may end up suffering for nothing. Shoes can become more comfortable with wear, but if they're not comfortable when you try them on in the store, chances are they never will be.

Sizing

It's surprising how many guys end up settling for a size smaller or a size larger than their proper fit, either because they're too lazy to go one store over, or wait an extra week for a new shipment, or because they just want to get the bloody shopping excursion over and done with. It is vital, however, that you get the right shoe size.

Finding the right shoe size, as you likely already know, is an eternal process. Different brands have different sizes; just because you're a 12 when it comes to your sneakers, it does not necessarily mean you're a 12 in your loafers. It's therefore a good idea to measure your foot each time you buy a pair of shoes or sneakers.

Don't depend on your wife, girlfriend, or buddy to measure your feet correctly—get help from a salesperson. And, although it sounds basic, be sure to stand up when the salesperson measures your feet. This will ensure that your feet are at their longest, and that you get the most accurate measurement.

Don't just try on one shoe. Remember that your feet are not always identical in size. Put both on your feet and walk around the store—treat this prospective purchase as you would a car: Nobody ever gets in the driver's seat, adjusts the mirror, and says, "I'll take it!" They go for a test-drive. Buy with your bigger foot in mind, and buy an insole to even out the two if the discrepancy is noticeable.

SHOE WIDTH

Everyone knows a 10 is bigger than a 9. But how many guys know that 2E is *wider* than D? Here's a quick guide to the sometimes-confusing terminology used to denote shoe width.

2A: Extra-Narrow
B: Narrow
D: Standard Width
2E: Wide
4E: Extra-Wide
6E: Extra, Extra-Wide

Heels and Toes

A key factor in getting the right shoe size is making sure your heels and toes fit snugly, without causing discomfort.

To know if your shoes are fitting correctly around your heel, use your index finger to fit between the shoe's heel and your heel. It should slide between them with relatively little force. If your finger cannot fit, the shoes are too tight. If your finger has too much room, the shoes are too large.

At the other end, your toes should be able to wiggle comfortably. You should be able to fit the width of your thumb in between the tips of your toes and the end of the shoe. Your mother probably used this "rule of thumb" test on you when you were a kid. And guess what? It still works.

Arch support

The curve of your foot's arch is hereditary, but there are a few things you can do to accommodate it.

If you have high arches (and therefore, inflexible feet), seek out well-cushioned, flexible shoes and a shoe with a curved instep.

People with no arch (a condition known as flat-footedness) may notice that their feet lean inward. This condition requires a shoe with a straight instep to keep it stable while walking or running.

People with regular foot arches are best off with a slightly curved instep. This will provide an optimum mix of stability and flexibility.

And when all else fails, head out to the local drugstore. There's an enormous range of inexpensive arch braces and orthotic supports out there that can be used to prevent discomfort.

Hallmarks of comfort

You've established that a pair of shoes fits you comfortably—in the store. But how do you ensure that they will continue to do so? There are certain visual indicators that a shoe's snug and cozy fit will persist. Here they are.

Breathable fabrics

When examining the upper part of the shoe (technically known as the tongue and vamp), look for high quality materials like high-end leathers or synthetic fabrics, which will allow your feet to breathe with ease. Walking around with sweaty feet all day can be really uncomfortable, and may make your feet smell like Parmesan cheese.

A softer upper portion is generally better unless you have problems with the balls of your feet. In that case, a slightly stiffer design is recommended to reduce the stress from your foot.

Smooth lining

The lining on the inside part of the shoe should be smooth and preferably seamless, to provide a more comfortable fit. Take a quick look inside the shoe to see whether its construction is solid, to avoid being faced with a lining that starts to rip and slip after two weeks.

Rounded soles

The soles of your shoes will spend the most face-time with concrete, so they deserve particular consideration. Flat soles are ideal, but most shoes slope gently upwards under the toes. For maximum comfort, opt for shoes with somewhat rounded outsoles; they'll encourage you to move off of the heel and onto the toes as you're walking.

Sturdy heels

Heels account for the largest proportion of the shoe's weight, and they help maintain your body's position. For that reason, you should choose shoes with a slightly wider heel area for extra balance and cushioning.

Research shows that heels approximately half an inch high are perfect since they'll help you avoid overstretching your Achilles tendons. Also, make an effort to look for shoes with sturdy heel counters (the leather strip on the back of the shoe) since they'll help you maintain good heel position when the shoe contacts the ground.

SHOE SHOPPING TIPS

■ For the best fit and selection, go to specialty dress shoe stores.

■ For the best deals, visit department stores, wholesalers, and outlet malls. Don't shy away from buying shoes or sneakers on clearance, either. The only thing these shoes are usually guilty of is being a season or two "out of style." But honestly, when you get out on the street, nobody can tell the difference between a 2005 Kenneth Cole oxford and a 2007 Kenneth Cole oxford.

■ If you are going to buy shoes online, a good trick is to try on the same pair in a store to ensure a comfortable fit, and then go online for the best deal. But if you have previous experience with a particular brand, then there's no need to worry about purchasing shoes online without trying them on first. In any case, most reputable online retailers offer full refunds.

■ Visit shoe stores on Sunday mornings, or late on weeknights. Chances are you will be the only customer in the store, and the salesperson will be able to concentrate on you. The result? Knowledgeable, one-on-one service.

SOCKS: THE BASICS

What are shoes without socks? More importantly, what are *feet* without socks? Foot and shoe moisture tend to attract fungi, viruses, and other bacteria. Clean socks are necessary not only for your own health, but also for your shoes' wellbeing.

Types of Socks

Socks fall into three main categories (not to mention the area between the wall and the dryer): Dress, casual, and athletic.

■ **Dress socks** are usually made from silk, cashmere, or fine variants of cotton and wool.

■ **Casual socks** come in cotton and wool, and are available in a wide variety of colors, patterns, and thicknesses.

■ **Athletic socks** are usually cotton and available in gray or white. This type differs most obviously from casual socks by virtue of their size. Athletic socks tend to come up to the mid-calf and higher, or simply right above the heel (ankle-length), making them invisible when wearing sneakers.

Your sock size should be 1 to 1.5 sizes bigger than your shoe size. Some brands divide sock size by small, medium, and large.

To know your size, refer to these numbers (in inches):
Medium: 5–9
Large: 9–12
Extra large: 13–15

Matching Socks

When wearing dress shoes, always match your socks to your pants. Matching your socks to your shoes will look a bit off, as if you're wearing adult booties. And given that you've already matched your shoes with your pants, you needn't worry about too wild a clash between them and your socks.

Once you've got basic sock matching down pat, you can start getting a little bolder. Start by seeking out socks with subtle patterns or multiple colors and match them with other elements in your outfit (even those from the waist up). For example, if you're wearing a black suit with a red tie and black shoes, you can wear black socks that feature a subtle red pattern. With tweed you might want to consider wearing earthy colors or pick one of the shades featured in the tweed pattern and opt for solid colored socks.

You should also know that, according to purists, socks should extend over your calves any time you're wearing a tie. This prevents any part of your bare leg from being exposed while seated, and puts an end to you occasionally having to pull up your socks, which is inexcusable.

---

5 SHOES EVERY GUY SHOULD OWN

The present rule tackles dress shoes in depth because they are the most perplexing and expensive to purchase, and therefore merit considerable reflection. But we know that your shoe rack doesn't start and end with your formal shoes. So, which shoe styles should be in your wardrobe? Here are five shoes that every man should have lined up in a neat little row on the floor of his closet, ready to complete an outfit for any occasion that might arise.

1. The sneaker

Casual wear is an important part of every man's lifestyle. You can't be in the office all the time, right? And for relaxing on the weekends, chances are you opt for a great pair of jeans and a laidback shirt. When you're in casual mode, be sure to adorn your feet accordingly by including a stylish sneaker in your shoe collection.

2. The casual shoe

Since not every laidback occasion is sneaker-appropriate, you're going to need a second type of casual shoe. This second footwear option comes in the form of a lace-up shoe with a thin leather sole. Today's casual shoes are sleek, structured, and void of any bulk, and will look immaculate paired with a straight-leg jean.

3. The black dress shoe

For those high-brow formal occasions, or for a regular day at work, the black dress shoe is a classic item of footwear to own. There are no exceptions to this rule. You can mix and match the many available styles of dress shoe with your slacks and suits.

4. The brown dress shoe

In today's fashion world, brown is the new black. While black is still a classic color and reserved for ultra-formal occasions, brown has become an acceptable alternative for occasions that are less decorous, yet still proper—like the boardroom, for example.

5. The ankle boot

The ankle boot is an important shoe to add to your collection—especially for the fall. It's a functional piece because you can wear it in varied ways. For instance, you can wear your ankle boot with a business suit or a pair of jeans and it will complement both looks successfully. A black leather, square-toe boot is an example of a sophisticated shoe that can be matched with almost any pair of pants.

CLASSIC DRESS SHOE STYLES

Now it's time to navigate through the ocean of different styles that will greet you at the shoe store. This is an intimidating venture, particularly as you're now aware how integral (and pricey) this purchase will be. Your best route is to stick with the classics. Here are four of the core dress shoe styles.

Oxfords

Originally known as Balmorals in England, oxfords are leather shoes with a relatively low instep, closed lacing, and a non-rubber sole. Modern oxfords, however, may be constructed from suede or synthetic materials, but no matter the material used to construct them, oxfords are usually quite plain with few—if any—embellishments.

Like most dress shoes, oxfords traditionally come in black, cordovan, brown, burgundy, oxblood, chestnut, and, occasionally, white. Oxfords are good all-around dress shoes that are appropriate for numerous occasions. For the office, basic, unadorned black oxfords will do the trick. Semiformal or contemporary chic events call for oxfords as well, though you can vary the color on these occasions, choosing shoes in shades such as cognac for a sophisticated but still down-to-earth feel. For formal affairs, revert to black oxfords made of highly polished, shiny leather, as well as heels and soles that are sleek and have as little bulk as possible.

The true classic and quintessentially British oxford is the cap-toe oxford. If you're going for simple, classic, and timeless, it doesn't get much more simple, classic, or timeless than this. Cap-toe shoes have an additional layer or band of leather over the toe. In their most traditional incarnation (the one illustrated above), this consists of a clean and simple line. Stylish and heavily decorated cap toes (such as the wing-tip brogue) are available, but these should be matched carefully and reserved for less stoic occasions.

Loafers

First making their appearance in the earlier part of the 20th century, loafers can be either dressy or worn as a dressy sport shoe (think yachting and you'll understand). The distinguishing feature of all loafers, however, is a lack of laces or buckles. Traditionally made from leather, loafers are slip-on shoes that resemble a moccasin on top, but have a wide and fairly flat heel. Many loafers have tassels, although these are often dispensed with nowadays. Penny loafers have a strap across the upper portion of the shoe, which was originally designed to hold change or an ornament.

Dress boots

Dress boots are slim, ankle-length boots with a slight heel that fits the foot and leg quite snugly. This style of boot is often highly polished and is frequently embellished with perforations. These boots will look fantastic with dressy and casual clothes, such as a great-fitting pair of dark-colored designer jeans, a pair of dress trousers, or a casual suit.

Monk strap

This term refers to dress shoes that are similar to loafers in that they don't have laces. While loafers are typically plain or tasseled, monk strap shoes have a metallic buckle and a leather strap on the upper portion of the shoe.

SHINE YOUR SHOES IN 5 EASY STEPS

There's nothing like stepping out in a squeaky clean pair of shoes and making a great first impression, both at the office and after hours. Take the extra time to make sure your shoes look clean and properly shone at all times.

Shining your shoes is a task that will take less than 30 minutes each time, and if you break down the cost of a good shoeshine kit and compare it to the number of times you'll be shining your shoes, you'll see that it's completely worth it in the long run.

The shoeshine kit

A complete shoeshine kit costs anywhere between $25 and $80, depending on the brand and quality of the shoe polish and brushes. Keep in mind that you usually get what you pay for—a first-rate shoeshine kit is sure to be long-lasting.

A typical shoeshine kit includes:

- A shoeshine and polish brush
- Shine or buffing cloths (a.k.a. chamois or shammy)
- A shoehorn
- Standard brown and black polish
- An all-purpose leather cleaner and conditioner

Shoeshine kit replacement

If you're on a tight budget, you can save some money by purchasing each component separately and making your own shoeshine kit. All you'll need are two brushes and some polish, and you can even replace the chamois with a cotton cloth, old T-shirt, sock, or dishrag.

Shine them in no time: 5 easy steps

1. Prevention

Better safe than sorry. Take the time to cover your work area with an old rag or newspapers in order to prevent polish stains on your floor. Also, try to be careful throughout your shine job—you don't want stains on your clothes either.

2. Start with a clean slate

Before smearing polish all over, make sure your shoes are free of dust and debris. Use a shoeshine brush or a wet cloth to carefully clean away the dust and grime. Wipe off any excess debris with your dry chamois or cotton cloth; just be careful not to scratch the leather.

3. Polish

Once your shoes are clean and dry, apply a sufficient amount of polish with your shoe polish brush. Spread it evenly over the surface of the shoe. For hard-to-reach areas, use a cotton swab or toothbrush. Wait 15 to 20 minutes for the polish to dry.

4. Back to work

Once your shoe is completely dry, use the shoeshine brush to meticulously wipe off the polish. Again, use a clean cotton swab or toothbrush for those hard-to-reach spots.

5. The finishing touch

Keep in mind that each and every step of the shoeshine process is important. However, they are all rendered useless if your buff job is subpar. Use a clean, lint-free shine cloth or chamois to give your shoes the shine they deserve. Buff the shoes using small, quick, circular strokes. That's all there is to it.

RULE 4
JEANS

In the same manner that we tend to neglect putting thought into purchasing collared shirts because we've been wearing them so long, we guys tend to bit a bit flippant in purchasing jeans because we've been hard-wired to see them as casual wear. And they are casual wear indeed, but they are also frequent wear—very frequent wear. For many of us, even daily wear.

Nevertheless, although we'll labor and agonize over purchasing a suit that we'll sport only a handful of times a year, we'll only dedicate 20 minutes to choosing a pair of jeans that will be worn a few times a week. That's an odd disconnect, and one that we'll remedy in the coming chapter as we guide you through the right way to select, try on, and purchase the kind of jeans that will mark you as a distinguished man in even the most casual setting.

JEAN FITS, CUTS, AND WASHES

The first step in shopping for a pair of jeans is learning the lay of the land. There are so many different types of jeans to choose from that finding the right pair for your body can be quite a daunting task. All three jean elements—fit (how the jeans sit on the body), cut (how the jeans are shaped), and wash (how the jeans are colored and finished)—must be accurately paired with your specific body type for a flawless, fashionable match. The good news is that for most average body types (like thin, athletic, or heavy-set) there is a perfect jean that will hide your flaws and accentuate your assets; all you need to know is how to find it.

Jean Fits

FIT	DESCRIPTION	APPROPRIATE BODY TYPE
Slim	Tight in the seat and thigh	Thin
Regular	Slim in the seat and thigh Loose in the legs	Athletic Thin
Relaxed	Loose in the seat and thigh without being baggy	Heavy-set Athletic
Loose	Very loose and baggy throughout seat, thigh and leg	Athletic

Jean Cuts

CUT	DESCRIPTION	AVAILABLE FITS	APPROPRIATE BODY TYPE
Boot cut (flare cut)	Tapers to the knee Slight flare at the bottom	Slim Regular	Thin Athletic Heavy-set
Skinny leg	Tight fit throughout the leg	Slim	Thin
Wide leg	Seat, thighs and leg are loose Leg is straight and slightly tapered from the thigh to the ankle	Relaxed Loose	Athletic Heavy-set

CUT	DESCRIPTION	AVAILABLE FITS	APPROPRIATE BODY TYPE
Straight leg	Uniform fit from the top of the leg to the bottom Bottom does not flare or taper	Slim Regular	Tall Thin
High rise	Sits on the natural waistline	Regular Relaxed Loose	Short
Low rise	Sits just below the natural waistline	Slim Regular Relaxed Loose	Tall Thin Athletic

Jean Washes

WASH	DESCRIPTION	APPROPRIATE BODY TYPE
Dark	Original denim color (deep blue) Jean is often rough and stiff	Thin Athletic Heavy-set
Stone	Denim is weathered Cotton is soft Color looks faded and worn	Thin Athletic
Dirty	Pre-washed for faded, worn-in look Tinged with a brown or khaki-like color to appear "dirty"	Thin Athletic Heavy-set
Distressed	Highly faded Often have holes, rips and frayed hems	Thin Athletic

MATCHING JEANS TO YOUR BODY

Our table addressed which jeans are appropriate for which generic body type, but this is a topic that deserves a bit more exploration. Let's take a deeper look at some of our cuts.

Straight cut

Straight-cut jeans typically sit at your natural waist and are slim through the seat and thighs. The fabric should skim your silhouette and the leg should be long, tapering off gradually and slightly at the ankle. This style of jean is classic, and if you have the body to wear them, straight-cut jeans can be paired with pretty much anything.

Flare cut

Also known as boot-cut jeans, and originally designed to be worn with cowboy boots, this cut is very flattering for many body types. Typically, flare-cut styles should sit just below your natural waist and should be slightly loose through the leg. From the knee to the ankle, these jeans become slightly wider or "flare" out. A bonus is that these jeans will never go out of style and it's easy to dress them up for a date or the office.

Wide leg

Like flared jeans, wide-leg jeans often sit at your natural waist or just below it, but the seat and thighs of these jeans will have a relaxed or loose fit. Back pockets may be larger and deeper on this style of jean. Wide-leg jeans usually have a straight, slightly tapered cut from the thigh to the ankle, but they are very loose through the leg so that the shape of your body is not as easily discernible.

Low rise

The defining feature of low-rise jeans is that they sit below your natural waistline, often on the hipbones. Low-rise jeans can be straight cut, slim fit, bootleg, or wide leg. It's best to wear low-rise jeans with a longer shirt, otherwise your midriff will be visible anytime you move your arms—while girls might be able to get away with belly-baring jeans and short T-shirts at the bar, this look is never a good one for men.

It's all in your jeans

Tall and lean

Straight-cut jeans will flatter this body type best. If you are blessed with a great physique, jeans with a flat front and a straight leg will show off your body to its best advantage. Boot-cut jeans are another option for this body type—particularly if you have wider hips—as a flared cut will balance your shape, creating a straighter, streamlined look. Tall and lean men can also carry off wide-leg jeans, but be aware that they will look very casual on this body type and are therefore better suited for weekends than for the office.

Slender

If you are slim and of average height, avoid jeans that adhere too closely to your body unless you like the starving-artist look. Steer clear of wide-leg jeans as well, as you risk looking lost in your clothes. For your most flattering look, choose straight-cut, low-rise jeans that sit comfortably and low on the hips with a couple of extra inches of room through the leg. Slightly flared jeans also flatter slender figures by creating the illusion of a better defined silhouette. For a more ample-looking rear, look for back pockets with flaps or extra material as this will add bulk to your behind.

Athletic

Athletic and muscular types look best in jeans with a wider leg since looser cuts show off the shape of a toned body. Jeans cut too close to the body are not as good a choice for muscular shapes as they can make muscles appear overly bulky. Wider-leg jeans, however, will subtly show off all your hard work at the gym. Additionally, to show off your butt or give it a more round shape, choose back pockets that are smaller and further apart.

Heavy-set

Larger frames should stay away from flare-cut jeans, as these tend to make heavier men appear larger. Wide-leg styles, however, are really great for concealing physical flaws. If there is a little more of you to love, this style will hide love handles and thick waists. Be careful not to choose styles that are too baggy, however, as they will make large bodies appear even larger. Instead, choose a loose shape with a few extra inches of room to show the shape of your body without hugging your frame too closely. Also bear in mind that larger, deeper pockets will make your butt look smaller and are therefore a good choice for heavier frames. Another way to conceal a larger behind is to look for pockets that are closer together.

A word to the wise: Once you find jeans that fit you perfectly, buy more than one pair. Get rid of other jeans that don't fit as well and replace your new jeans with a reserved pair about once a year when they fade and the bottoms become scruffy.

CARING FOR YOUR JEANS

Wash the jeans before hemming them

Washing before hemming will put the denim through any initial shrinking before you take more away. Just to be safe though, take off a little less than necessary when having them hemmed. If you need an inch taken off, go for two-thirds of an inch instead, which will buffer any future shrinkage.

Wash the jeans inside out

The first time you wash your jeans, wash them alone. After that, it's a good idea to wash them inside out, as this is the best possible way to maintain their color and overall look.

Don't put them in the dryer

If you're willing to go the extra mile, you should always lay your jeans on a towel to dry or, if possible, hang them with clothespins so that no part of the jeans is folded over.

UNDERSTANDING DENIM

The versatility of denim has made it one of the most popular styles of casual pants in fashion history. It seems, however, that denim's popularity has also made it a complicated item to shop for. To make the denim shopping experience a little less worrisome for our readers, AskMen.com sought the insight of jeans expert Jarrid Adler, who has worked with denim and the clothing business for over 15 years. Here are a few of the valuable points he had to offer.

On the price range of jeans:

"They're priced differently because there are so many components and factors that go into making a pair of jeans. For example, there are quality levels within the fabric. There is one fiber that goes in one direction and another fiber that goes in another direction; that's called the warp and weft. Sometimes these fibers are made by regular spinning cotton and some fibers are made with a special spindle called a ring spun, which spins the cotton unevenly and gives the finished fabric more character and depth, [making it] a more expensive and more authentic procedure.

"This is followed by the cost of cutting the fabric, sewing all the pieces together, and adding the trimming (buttons, zippers, rivets, embroidery, pockets, belt loops, etc.). Even within these trimmings there are some companies that use nickel rivets and buttons, which are the cheapest, but recently one company used 18-karat gold-plated buttons to jazz up their jeans, which definitely made a huge difference in the cost.

"Finally, there is the washing, which is usually the lion's share of the cost. Only certain procedures can be done by machine, and everything else has to be done by hand. For example, if you see a pair of jeans that has a certain whisker or marking that is truly original from [one pair of] jeans to the other, it means that it's done by hand. So there's some person in whatever factory physically making a scratch or making a hole on each individual pair of denim, and you've got to pay that person and that's where the labor costs come in . . . The more processes on the jean, the more expensive the washing factor is going to be. So it can get quite expensive when you talk about having a destroyed jean [because] somebody in the factory has to rip it with some sort of machine, wash it and rip it again, wash it, rip it again . . .

"Every little detail adds extra cost to the manufacturing and, inevitably, the quality of the product."

On shelling out for a good pair:

"If you're not somebody who wears a suit on a daily basis, you'll probably wear the suit about 10 to 12 times over the year. Buy a pair of jeans, and you'll probably wear them 50 times over the year. If you actually look at the cost-per-use, if you only wore the suit pants 10 times, which alone cost about $400, that's about $40 for every wear. If you spend $400 on a pair of jeans you wore 50 times, it only costs you $8 for every wear. In essence, if you look at that aspect, you're probably better off spending more money on a good pair of jeans that fits you well and that is superior in quality."

ESSENTIAL DENIM

It's becoming increasingly rare nowadays to find a workplace that demands a suit be worn on a daily basis. Though jeans were once relegated to weekend or outdoor activities, the casual office dress code means that denim has become the new uniform for life: It can be worn at work, at play, and everywhere in between. As much as this evolution has elevated our daily comfort levels, it also begets the uncomfortable question: Which jeans should I wear when?

Everyday jeans

Everyone should own a pair or two of simple, low-maintenance blue jeans. Why? Well for starters, most of us can't afford to drop over $250 a pop to be clad in the latest designer denim every day. Furthermore, some days we don't necessarily feel like sporting up-to-the-minute jeans. We just want to slip into our good ol' favorite pair of blue jeans and chill. You know that pair, the one that offers a no-headache solution day in and day out, and that you just can't get rid of because they're so comfortable.

Another reason why you should stock up on classic blue jeans is because it's usually harder to tell one pair apart from another, so you can wear them two or three days in a row without people noticing . . . a perfect excuse to delay laundry day.

So what exactly can be considered everyday jeans? In general, this category consists of any straight, relaxed (looser), or boot-cut pair that features four traditional pockets, a zipper or button-fly, and standard loopholes, and is available in traditional colors (various shades of blue, and the in-again, out-again blacks and grays). Everyday jeans should also feature minimal detailing. Avoid flashy stitching, excessive sandblast or dye treatments, pronounced front mustaches (bleached lines that contribute to a washed-out look), patchwork, and rips or frays. As a rule of thumb, your classic jeans should be simple, so try to avoid unnecessary bells and whistles.

You can find a decent pair of no-name classic jeans for as little as $40.

Jeans du jour

Mixing up your regular-priced jeans with a couple of splurge-worthy designer jeans will increase the versatility of your wardrobe. As with the rest of your wardrobe, however, you want this investment to be a wise one. And that means finding that delicate balance between trendiness and timelessness.

Dropping big bucks on a pair of jeans so trendy they'll look ridiculously dated in a year's time is completely absurd. At the same time, you want them to be distinguishable from your everyday jeans; a clear product of the present fashion climate.

Finding this balance is largely a matter of turning to the right provider. The labels that follow have sustained their status as trendsetters for several years now, and will likely continue to do so. Choose your pricey denim from among their offerings, and the amount of wear you get out of them will more than justify your investment.

Gucci

It's hard to get any more suave than Gucci. Their jeans look great on nearly everybody in addition to being completely appropriate for any occasion, save the most formal.

Paul Smith

Made in Japan and woven on an antique loom, jeans by British designer Paul Smith have an irregular finish that will become super comfortable over time. In a dark, natural indigo color, they will match all your casual and dress shirts and will mellow with a lot of wear to yield a lovely patina.

Edwin

Though not technically considered designer denim in Japan, from where Edwin hails, this label has developed a cult-like following stateside, and a pair of these is hot property. Edwin jeans are cut to flatter pretty much everybody and are extremely comfortable. Think of them as the cooler Japanese cousin to your favorite pair of Levi's.

7 for All Mankind

If you can't be bothered to spend hours at the gym, just pick up a pair of this label's jeans to make your legs and your butt look out of this world. A hint of Lycra in the fabric allows the jeans to really move with your body.

Diesel

A touch different from most jeans, but not so crazy that your friends will be able to spot you a mile away, Diesel jeans will instantly make you look stealthily hipper. In a dark blue color, you can wear them with almost anything, and everything you pair them with will be highlighted, thanks to their subtly quirky details. Diesel is a superstar when it comes to making slick, fashion-forward pieces, so you'll be in good hands with a pair of their downtown jeans with an uptown edge.

JAPANESE DENIM

Recent years have witnessed a lot of fuss from the fashion world over Japanese denim. A lot of it has to do with the sheer snob appeal of the idea of Japanese denim, and its most vocal proponents can typically substantiate their love of it no better than they could their fondness for Cuban cigars. As we're building you into a style maven from the inside out, let's ensure that you're one of the few who actually knows what he's talking about when the topic next arises.

Japanese culture is famous for its attention to detail, and jeans are no exception. Japanese denim has a cult following in Europe and America because of its amazing look and feel. It's different because it uses traditional production techniques that have long been abandoned elsewhere. Though far more labor-intensive—and expensive—jeans produced this way have a feel and appearance that is second to none.

Evisu was one of the first Japanese denim labels to become famous outside of Japan in the early '90s. The brand's founder, Hidehiko Yamane, was a self-confessed "jeans otaku" and bought vintage Levi's looms to produce his artisanal denim. Other brands use similar production methods to achieve a cloth that is stiffer, denser, and yet far more comfortable than the mass-produced denim used overseas.

One of the most distinctive characteristics of classic Japanese jeans is their "selvage edge," meaning that the fabric edges have a woven finish rather than being cut and overlocked like ordinary jeans. The selvage can be seen on the outer leg seam when cuffs are rolled up—a detail that will be noticed by denim connoisseurs and is a sign of the fabric's superior quality. Another factor in this quality is the dye used for Japanese denim: natural rather than synthetic indigo, with yarn dipped up to thirty times to produce an incredibly deep and rich color that weathers with time.

The reputation of Japanese denim has traveled quickly, and several overseas brands have adopted it for their collections. Cult Swedish brand Nudie uses Japanese denim for all its lines, and Diesel uses it for some of its premium jeans in response to demand for heavy, dense denim from shoppers. Paul Smith's Red Ear label uses Japanese denim and also styling details and stitching inspired by Japanese streetwear.

Like their manufacturers, Japanese consumers are also sticklers for detail, and the jeans worn on the streets of Tokyo reflect this. Trends in men's denim include the skinny cut, embellishment, and distressed wash. The skinny cut can be seen all over the city, usually in a dark wash and worn long enough to bunch around the ankles.

Embellishment takes many forms, from embroidery to chains and elaborate stitching. Evisu jeans are famous for their seagull mark across the back, which constantly morphs into new colors and sizes. Dark wash has been popular for several seasons, but its popularity is being challenged by faded, distressed denim, which can be seen everywhere on the streets of Shibuya, Tokyo's youth center.

In other cities, jeans are seen as a fashion fallback that can be pulled on without thinking, but Tokyo's trendsetters see denim as a matter for careful consideration, and they are willing to pay more for the perfect pair. And so, it seems, are a growing number of international denim fanatics who feed their habit through overseas stockists and eBay, and who swear that once you've tried Japanese denim, you can never, ever, go back.

Q&A

Getting girly

Dear AskMen.com,

I wanted to know your take on wearing girl's jeans. I'm a tall, lanky guy (6'1"), and I have pretty long, skinny legs. I started wearing jeans for women because I like the fit better than jeans for men, which happen to fall off my rear quite often. The girl jeans I wear don't look too bad. Do you think it's wrong for me to do so and could you perhaps point me in the right denim direction?

Joe

Joe,

We'll only say this once: Step away from the girl jeans. The beauty of denim is that it comes in a variety of styles, fits, and sizes, so even a "tall, lanky" guy such as yourself can find a pair that fits him like a glove.

Skinny jeans for both men and women have become quite the rage recently, so if it's a fitted leg and glammed-up style you're after, try the skinny jean out. If you want a more conventional cut, go with a straight-leg jean; anything baggier will make a thin guy look like he's swimming in his denim.

AskMen.com

RULE 5
COORDINATE

Roughly halfway into AskMen.com's *Style Bible*, you've already acquired a great deal of fashion knowledge. In fact, your style savvy already outstrips that of 90% of the male population, and you've probably already enjoyed the rewards of that knowledge if you've applied it in a recent shopping excursion.

But let's not start applauding ourselves just yet. You've got the basics down; now it's time to take your fashion sense to the next level. You know the ins and outs of matching garments to your own body type and sense of style, and we'll continue to refine that knowledge. But we're also going to add another layer of complexity to the mix, and start training you to match those same garments with one another. Your crash course in coordination will begin with colors.

5 RULES FOR WEARING COLOR

Sticking to a drab palette of black, gray, blue, and the occasional khaki-colored neutral is a route that many men take, because it's the safe one.

It's also the bland one, and an approach that you can abandon in light of your newfound knowledge and confidence.

Wearing color can be a tricky thing for men, but a few splashes here and there will enhance all the clothes you already own and ensure that you stand stylishly apart from the crowd. Here are some rules to apply as you begin to incorporate color into your wardrobe.

1. Use color to accessorize

Color need not be restricted to core wardrobe items, and in many cases, these shouldn't be colorful at all. After all, you want your core staples to be timeless, enduring ones, and colors can prove an obstacle to this.

Colored accessories, on the other hand, are a great way to show your playful side. A brightly colored belt is a fast, inexpensive, and easy way to enhance all your existing outfits. Bright blue, green, and red belts are all great additions for those individuals who are a little wary of wearing color. Pair these bright beauties with jeans and a white collared shirt for a casual-yet-hip look during the day. To spice up your evening wear, add the belt to a slim-cut black suit or team it with jeans and a dark blazer.

2. Wear one bold piece at a time

One bold piece of color can be incredibly eye-catching, but more than one will simply leave you looking like a clown. A forest green trench coat worn with brazen attitude looks impeccably stylish when paired with denim or khaki trousers. The important thing to remember when wearing dominant pieces of color is that the rest of your outfit should be confined to neutrals and basic cuts—so, no frilly tuxedo shirts.

3. Spend more for color

Did your father ever sit you down and tell you never to wear fuchsia? Well he's wrong, because if it happens to be in the form of an extravagantly expensive cashmere sweater, you most certainly can. Essentially, the more outrageous the color, the better the quality of the fabric in— and the higher the price of—your garment should be. Note: A $10 hot-pink shirt looks like a $2 hot-pink piece of crap.

4. Layer your colors

If you're afraid of making too bold a statement with a colored shirt or sweater, don't be afraid of testing the waters by layering your look a bit. In the colder months, wear a dark blazer over a colored shirt or sweater for a sporty, European look. For spring and summer, be casually cool by layering a white polo shirt over a brightly colored, long-sleeve cotton crewneck.

5. Keep it all in the family

Don't be afraid to wear two colored pieces at once; just remember to keep them in the same color family. For example, wearing a printed shirt with a solid-colored tie that picks up your shirt's color goes a long way in showing girls you can pick an outfit.

MATCHING COLOR TO YOUR COMPLEXION

Whether you're dark-skinned, medium-toned, or pale-skinned, you can find appropriate colors for your complexion.

Dark skin tone

Dark-skinned men tend to have black or dark brown hair and eyes. If you fall into this category, the colors that you wear should contrast with your dark features. The contrast brightens up your look and catches the eye.

Colors you look your best in:

- pink

- white

- khaki

- baby blue

- gray

Colors you should avoid:

- black

- dark brown

- turquoise

- spring green

- magenta

You should stay away from tropical colors and really dark shades. While black and navy blue are hard to avoid altogether because they basically make up the corporate uniform, try to keep them to a minimum and wear only when necessary.

Medium skin tone

Medium-toned men can have anything from blonde locks to jet-black manes, and their eye color can vary from baby blue to onyx black. If you're lucky enough to fall into this category, it means that you can wear just about any color and still look sharp. Since light and dark colors both contrast nicely with your skin tone, you can go either way.

Colors you look your best in:

- beige

- burgundy

- royal blue

- navy

- black

- pink (stripes)

Colors you should avoid:

- pistachio

- mauve

- dark brown

- red

- olive

The only colors that you should really avoid are those that might blend in too closely with your skin tone. For example, if you have an olive complexion, avoid wearing olive-colored or brown clothing.

Pale skin tone

Pale-skinned men will tend to have red, blonde, or dirty blonde hair. Their eye color is often just as fair, including green, blue, gray, or hazel. If you match this description, your best bet is to go with more subdued colors and pastels. These will blend well with your skin tone, and create a look that's both appealing and relaxing to the eye.

Colors you look your best in:

- light blue

- brown

- beige

- off white

- bold blue

Colors you should avoid:

- red

- pink

- orange

- yellow

- purple

The key is to steer clear of harsh or bright colors since these will contrast with your skin in an unflattering way. Basically, your clothes will stand out while you fade into the background. That said, stay away from vibrant colors at all costs.

Q&A

Is white all good?

Dear AskMen.com,
Is it true that white works best for people with a certain physique and complexion?

Steve

Steve,

White works well with most skin complexions. However, if you haven't been out in the sun for a while, then wearing all white might not be the most flattering option for your skin tone. Instead, try to contrast your lighter features with brighter colors like red, pale blue, yellow, light orange, and even some earth tones like beige.

In terms of physique, white tends to emphasize most body parts, so if you're on the heavy side, then you might want to wear less white, especially around your problem areas. So, for example, if you're heavier around the waist and gut, then avoid wearing white—especially white pants, because they will make your bottom look larger, drawing people's eyes away from your charming smile and straight to your belly.

AskMen.com

WHAT COLOR SAYS ABOUT YOU

Different colors are known to embody different energetic vibrations, and they can express and reflect a range of characteristics and emotions. When wearing color, it's helpful to know the kind of subliminal messages you are projecting through your outfit—especially when it comes to the ladies.

Red

The color red evokes dominance, power, and attention. Red clothing will definitely make you stand out from the rest of the crowd and will mark you with sexual energy. Red is a commanding color that should be worn once in a while, for those times when you really want to make a statement and be different.

Peach/Pink

Peach and pink project an upbeat attitude and calming characteristics, as well as good health. While some men shun pink as a less-than-manly option, the fact is that it is completely acceptable, generally flattering, and wearing it may in fact make you look more masculine, since it shows that you are confident enough in yourself to not be defined by outdated color codes.

Black

The color of darkness is undoubtedly the most popular color in fashion. A man wearing black suggests elegance, authority, and power. When worn properly, black clothing also conveys neatness, simplicity, and great versatility.

White

White clothing is a sign of virtue and can give you an extremely clean appearance. This obviously implies that your white clothing should be spotless. White clothing can also point towards a higher social status, and looks very preppy.

Blue

Blue clothing suggests a more trustworthy and warm personality. Blue garments can also make you look more serious and intellectual.

Yellow

Yellow clothing is very visually stimulating. It conveys anxiety and alertness, as well as optimism.

Burgundy

Burgundy clothing and fashion accessories convey passion and high spirituality. They're also a sign of higher status and luxury.

Gray

Finally, gray clothing and fashion accessories emit a touch of class, and can make you look efficient and brainy. Gray is a neutral color that is easily matched with most other hues. Needless to say, most clothing and fashion accessories look great in gray, and its versatility is a bonus.

MAKING SENSE OF PATTERNS

Once you've got a handle on the colors that suit you, you can throw patterns into the mix. Patterns are intimidating because they often need to be matched, and there has to be solid knowledge guiding that matching. If you match your patterns haphazardly, you may emerge from your wardrobe really looking like a crazy person.

You could play it safe and stick with solid colors forever, but then you will never distinguish yourself as a well-dressed man. Instead, learn. Before you attempt to start matching patterns, it will help to know a bit more about what you're working with. Here are definitions of the 10 most popular patterns.

Houndstooth

A pattern of broken, jagged checks, said to resemble the bared teeth of a dog. And it kind of does, viewed from a distance with a squint.

Where you'll find it: In its small-sized variations, houndstooth is often used in men's jackets and, formerly, hats (think back to Coach Paul Bryant at the University of Alabama). Medium- and large-sized houndstooth checks abounded in women's coats and skirts in the '60s, and enjoyed a revival in the early '00s.

Herringbone

An alternating pattern between diagonal lines running to the right and diagonal lines running to the left. The result is an inverted V design, or one which, when viewed horizontally, looks like a cartoon fish bone.

Where you'll find it: Jackets, suits, and scarves. Herringbone is also a popular design in both men's and women's jewelry, and occasionally in floor tiling.

Windowpane check

A simple and rather bland pattern of open, plain squares. Uninteresting on its own, windowpane begs to be matched with another pattern.

Where you'll find it: Most commonly, on men's dress shirts.

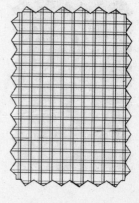

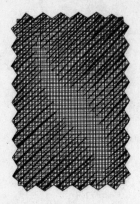

Sharkskin

Two different colored fabrics—one light and one dark—are woven across one another. The resulting pattern reflects light differently at shifting angles, allowing it to shine, much like a well-scrubbed shark.

Where you'll find it: This subtle pattern lends itself well to suits.

Barleycorn

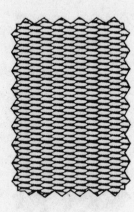

An assemblage of miniature, blurred ovals or triangles that resemble a cornfield (kind of). Often employed with tweed, lambswool, and other woolen fabrics.

Where you'll find it: In keeping with its usual host fabrics, on sports jackets and outdoors wear. Close your eyes and envision yourself hunting pheasant in the English countryside. Now look at the jacket you're wearing. It's barleycorn.

Pinstripe

Fine stripes, typically light on a dark background, are regularly spaced apart.

Where you'll find it: Pinstripe has become a classic suit pattern.

Chalkstripe

Blurry, wider pinstripes. The name derives from their appearing as if drawn by a piece of chalk.

Where you'll find it: Suits, trousers, and often in flat caps.

Paisley

An intricate design composed of swirling pinecone- or teardrop-like figures, giving rise to endless variations.

Where you'll find it: Paisley makes frequent appearances in bedsheets, drapes, furniture covers, and other textiles. In the '80s, solid-colored paisley bandannas found favor among L.A. gang members. Today, the only acceptable venue for paisley in a man's closet is on his tie rack or in his stack of pocket squares.

Nailhead check

Also known as bird's eye check, a pattern of dots so small as to produce the illusion of a single, solid color.

Where you'll find it: Because of its simplicity, nailhead lends itself to all manner of garments. You'll often see it in warm winter sweaters.

Glen check or plaid

Small checks alternate and overlap with large squares. Typically gray throughout. The full name of this pattern is Glenurquhart check; another widely and incorrectly applied name for it is Prince of Wales check. While the Prince (the one who would become Edward VII) did indeed design a check almost identical to the Glenurquhart, his was distinctive by virtue of its larger size and infusion of red and brown colors.

Where you'll find it: Suits, outdoor wear, and, in days gone by, fedoras.

---

4 RULES FOR MATCHING SHIRT AND TIE PATTERNS

Learning to combine patterned shirts and ties is not as taxing as it sounds. Just stick to a few simple rules and you'll find that mixing them is easy as can be.

1. Repeat colors in each pattern

In this case, choose your shirt first, carefully noting the dominant colors. When you are ready to pick your tie, choose one with accents that use the same dominant colors as your shirt.

2. Graduate checks outward

Skillfully combining a checked shirt with a differently checked tie is a quick way to get a distinct look. The rule to follow in this case is to always wear smaller checked prints on your body and larger checks around your neck. Again, make sure you pay attention to color and choose a shirt and tie in a similar color palette, and remember to keep your trousers in the same overall color scheme.

3. Vary weights between patterns

Choosing two patterns of the same size will just look too busy and confusing, so for a cleaner look that's easier on the eyes, make sure one piece has a chunkier pattern than the other.

4. Match smaller patterns with larger ones

You'll be surprised at the fantastic and elegant combinations you can come up with, even when the tie and shirt have completely different patterns, simply by following this rule. If your shirt has a small pattern, you'll need to wear a tie with a larger one, and vice versa. You don't even have to worry much about keeping to the same color family if the shirt is in a neutral color like black, gray, or white, although matching these pieces when the shirt is colored does make it easier to get it right.

MATCHING JACKETS AND PANTS

Buying separate jackets and trousers can be a daunting feat for the modern man. With so many jacket styles and trouser fits to choose from, a mismatch is bound to occur every now and again. The following is a lesson on how to avoid an embarrassing jacket and trouser mismatch.

Trouser fabric

The key to matching jackets and pants is not only in the color, as many men may think, but also in the fabric.

1. Flannel

The flannel trouser is the most versatile as it can be worn throughout a good part of the year and matches with a wide variety of jacket and blazer fabrics.

Recommended jacket: Tweed, corduroy

2. Wool gabardine

Wool trousers are smoother than flannel, and look best when paired with blazers of a contrasting fabric.

Recommended jacket: Tweed

3. Cotton corduroy

While warmer than flannel or wool, cotton corduroy trousers are best worn in the colder months and should be paired with an equally warm jacket.

Recommended jacket: Soft wool, cashmere

4. Chinos

Made of a predominantly cotton canvas, chinos are a casual trouser and their dressed-down style should be accurately reflected in the jacket they're paired with.

Recommended jacket: Corduroy

Trouser color

Now that you understand the importance of matching fabric when pairing trousers with jackets and blazers, understanding color is the final step in creating the perfect ensemble.

1. Vary colors

The most important rule to remember when matching jackets and trousers is to create contrast. For example, never wear gray trousers with a similarly colored gray jacket. Instead, opt for different shades of brown or blue.

2. Match tones

An important color-coordinating rule that is often misunderstood is that color *tones* must be matched rather than the actual colors themselves. In other words, the colors of the trousers and jacket have to "go" with each other rather than be carbon copies of each other. So, you could match different shades of the same color, or match soft tones with other soft tones to create the perfect color-coordinated ensemble. For example, wear a light blue button-down shirt under a dark blue V-neck sweater for a variation in shades, or combine a chocolate brown pair of trousers with a navy blue sport jacket for a soft-on-soft look.

3. Match colors from patterns

When matching jackets and trousers, you don't have to stick to solids. Throwing in a subtly patterned trouser or jacket not only adds some dimension to your getup, but also gives you more color to play with. If your blazer has a slight check pattern, for example, you can match the trousers with the color tone of the jacket itself or with a color in the check pattern.

A perfect match

Matching jackets and trousers is much more complicated than finding two colors that work together; you need to take the season along with its accompanying fabrics into consideration. Follow these guidelines, and your top and bottom will be properly outfitted for any casual occasion.

MATCH DRESS PANTS WITH SHOES

Men should follow these basic color combinations when deciding which shoes to wear with a pair of pants, regardless of whether they're dressy or not.

There are a bunch of other colors that could be thrown into the mix, but we'll keep it simple.

Shoe and Pants Color Guide

PANT/SUIT COLOR	SHOE COLOR
Black	black, tan or camel (a more risqué choice), oxblood
Gray	black, oxblood, camel
Brown	any shade of brown, black, camel
Navy	black, camel, tan, oxblood
Earth tones	any shade of brown, camel, black

A Guide to Dress Shoes

As for specific types of shoes to wear with specific styles of pants, here are a few suggestions:

Wear your khakis with . . .

1. For a classic look, wear your khakis with a pair of loafers to achieve traditional American business style. Another sure bet are simple oxfords.

2. For a preppy look, wear khakis with a slick pair of penny loafers.

Wear your 4-pocket pants and dress pants with . . .

1. For a more casual look, step into a handsome pair of monk strap shoes; their subtle buckle will give you a refined European look.

2. For the typical American businessman look, wear your dress pants with a pair of loafers or oxfords.

3. More casual 4-pocket pants can be paired with loafers or dress boots.

Wear your suits with . . .

1. Solid color: Every man should own a pair of black leather cap-toe lace-up oxfords; they're a staple in any professional wardrobe.

2. Pinstripe: Pinstripes evoke a sharper and bolder air; you don't want to compromise it with stuffy or clunky looking shoes. Instead, opt for a black wing-tip brogue, a lower heeled version of the traditional oxford that is distinct by virtue of its decorative perforations.

3. Trendy: Finally, ankle boots with a square or elongated pointy toe are riding high if you're seeking up-to-the-minute style.

Q&A

Loafer Don't

Dear AskMen.com,
I have a pair of black loafers and light khaki shorts, and I wanted to know if I could wear the two together. Also, what kind of socks and what color socks do I wear with them?

Nick

Hi Nick,
Unless you want to look like a middle-aged country-club hopper, don't pair the loafers with the shorts. Save the loafers for regular-length pants, and when you do find an appropriate time for them, stick to solid black socks.

AskMen.com

Chocolate brown suit

Dear AskMen.com,
I have a dark chocolate brown suit. I'm convinced that black is the most appropriate shoe color for this suit. In fact, anything brown in the local

stores' shoe departments would look obscene, in my opinion. My girl-friend, however, disagrees. In her mind, a brown suit equals brown shoes only. Please settle this debate.

Jonathan

Jonathan,

You're both right, but in this case we have to favor your girlfriend's opinion—sorry to break it to you, dude. Although black shoes can complement a dark chocolate brown suit adequately, a pair of light brown dress shoes will complete the look flawlessly. If the dress code at your office allows it, we'd even recommend that you wear your dark brown suit with a classy pair of beige or camel dress shoes.

AskMen.com

6 RULES OF LAYERING

Layering is a great way to combine your favorite pieces and wear something comfortable and flexible while showcasing your sense of style. It's also very practical; you can slip on an extra layer in the morning when it's still crisp outside, remove it in the afternoon once it heats up, and then slip it back on when the temperature drops after sunset. But it can also be quite daunting: Every layer should align with the surrounding ones, but still be presentable enough to display alone if you need to shed a few.

Here are six basic guidelines to see you through layering properly.

1. Thinner clothes first

The first rule is straightforward and logical: the closer to your skin, the thinner the material. That said, make sure to start with items that are made from thinner fabrics such as a cotton T-shirt, dress shirt, or turtleneck, and then layer them with heavier items such as a wool sweater, a corduroy blazer, or a leather jacket.

2. Keep it casual

Layering is best used for casual occasions and is generally not appropriate in more formal settings. Keep in mind, however, that a layered combo can include one or more classy pieces, such as a tailored blazer and a fine dress shirt.

3. Always feel comfortable

As a general rule, you shouldn't wear anything that feels uncomfortable. With that in mind, if you can't put your arms all the way down to your sides or scratch the back of your ear, then your layering combination is most likely too thick, and therefore, far from trendy.

4. Mix in some color

Just because the mercury drops, it doesn't mean you have to put a freeze on your color selection. Black, brown, navy, and gray are all great fall/winter colors, but so are lime green, purple, and fuchsia . . . well, at least when worn and combined properly. Brightly colored pieces make for excellent middle layers, peeping out from between more muted layers to give your outfit an intriguing flair. Be fearless and don't hesitate to spice up your look with a little color.

5. Be practical in layering

In general, you're better off wearing two or three thinner layers of clothing rather than one thick one—especially during fall, when the weather can fluctuate drastically.

6. Jacket not required

Last but not least, remember that layering does not necessarily include a jacket. A couple of thinner layers, a warm sweater, and a scarf will easily see you through a cool fall day.

RULE 6
ACCESSORIZE

Nowhere is the gender gap in fashion knowledge more evident than in the realm of accessories. It's evident in the way we shop: While women are off considering the merits of scarves, jewelry, and other accessories, we guys are typically laps behind them, agonizing over whether a sweater will match with our jeans. It's something akin to her putting the final seasonings on a gourmet omelet while we're still figuring out how to fry the egg.

This discrepancy is the simple product of different style upbringings: Women are attuned to the finer points of fashion by virtue of prolonged exposure to fashion magazines and commentary, whereas men end up playing catch-up later in life. It's definitely worth catching up on your knowledge of accessories. Their value resides in:

1. Their versatility. One accessory lends itself to pairing with a host of different garments.

2. Their economic availability. Most accessories, even those that come from top-notch labels, are relatively inexpensive.

3. Their visual impact. Sport a pair of cufflinks or a pocket square, and you're showcasing your style confidence—as you should.

We'll start our investigation into accessories with one that has become commonplace male attire: the tie. We've addressed the art of matching ties with other garments, now let's look at a dimension of the tie that almost comprises an accessory in itself—the tie knot.

MASTER DIFFERENT TIE KNOTS

For many men, wearing a tie is about as much fun as wearing a noose around the neck. Some men will even shun formal events simply to avoid wearing one. Could likening a tie to a noose have something to do with the fact that so many men have limited skills when it comes to dealing with ties? Even if you went to a private school and wore a uniform every day of your adolescent life, you still probably only know how to tie one kind of knot. And as for everybody else, well, your dad probably showed you once and then left you to your own devices.

Well, when it comes to learning to knot a tie in different ways, it's better late than never—and it's knowledge that will always be pertinent. Let's guide you through the four classic ways to knot a tie as well as the occasions for which each type of knot is appropriate. Who knows? By the time you're finished reading this section, you may even feel confident enough to wear a tie just for fashion's sake.

Windsor

Often erroneously referred to as the "double Windsor" due to the existence of the half Windsor knot, the Windsor is the most traditional—and perhaps the most intimidating—knot. This type of knot is all-purpose, and is appropriate for business meetings, interviews, and anywhere else you need to look respectable. Because it produces a rather wide knot, however, you'll only want to pair it with wide spread collars.

Here are the steps to tying a Windsor knot:

1. Place the tie around your neck with the skinny end hanging on one shoulder and the fat end on the other shoulder. The fat end should hang roughly a foot lower than the thin end.

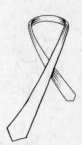

2. Cross the fat portion over the skinny end to make an X fairly close to your neck (at around about the second button on your shirt).

3. Loop the fat end underneath the thin end and up through the neck loop. Drop it down so it overlaps the thin end again.

4. Pull the fat end behind the bundle of cloth you have created (your first step toward the final knot) to the left. Pull it up and drop it down through the neck loop again, then pull it to the left again.

5. Pull the fat end over from left to right, overlapping your evolving knot.

6. Pull the fat end up through the loop again, behind what now looks like a nearly-complete knot.

7. Bring the fat end back down and insert it through the knot.

8. Finish your knot by tightening it. In doing so, you will see the beginnings of a natural dimple form. Manipulate it manually to make this dimple as distinct as possible. Its purpose is to add depth to an otherwise flat, bland-surfaced tie, and concurrently to mark you as a man of style. You will never leave the house without a dimple in your tie again.

Half-Windsor

The half-Windsor offers the upscale look of a Windsor with less effort. Accordingly, there's a good chance that you'll come to rely on it pretty heavily. It's not as wide as the Windsor, but its still wide enough that you should make sure it's not pushing your collar up awkwardly.

1. Place the tie around your neck with the skinny end hanging on one shoulder and the fat end on the other shoulder. The fat end should hang roughly a foot lower than the thin end.

2. Cross the fat portion over the skinny end to make an X fairly close to your neck (at around about the second button on your shirt).

3. Pull the fat end behind the thin end to the right, then up in front of it and down through the neck loop.

4. Pull the fat end over from left to right, overlapping your evolving knot.

5. Pull the fat end up through the loop again, behind what now looks like a nearly-complete knot.

6. Bring the fat end back down and insert it through the knot.

7. Finish your knot by tightening it. Again, accentuate that dimple.

Four-in-hand

Learn this knot and use it when you need to look good in a rush, or when you want to be fashionable and wear a tie with casual clothes. Try combining this type of knot with a dress shirt that has a narrow collar opening and is made from a softer material.

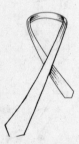

1. Place the tie around your neck with the skinny end hanging on one shoulder and the fat end on the other shoulder. The fat end should hang roughly a foot lower than the thin end.

2. Cross the fat portion over the skinny end to make an X fairly close to your neck (at around about the second button on your shirt).

3. Wrap the fat end around the thin end, then up through the neck loop. Drop the fat end back down and through the knot.

4. Finish your knot by tightening it. Note that the dimple is much harder to produce on this kind of knot, and may prove entirely elusive.

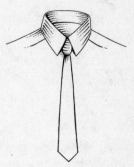

Pratt

Also known as the Shelby, this knot is highly symmetrical, like the Windsor, but looser to wear and not as time-consuming to create. Since the Pratt is neither as large as the Windsor nor as narrow as the four-in-hand knot, it pairs well with most dress shirts and looks suitable on any occasion.

1. Place the tie around your neck with the seam (the end with the tag) facing outward on both the thin and fat ends. Note that the fat end should be hanging lower than the thin end on your chest.

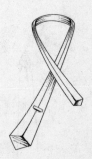

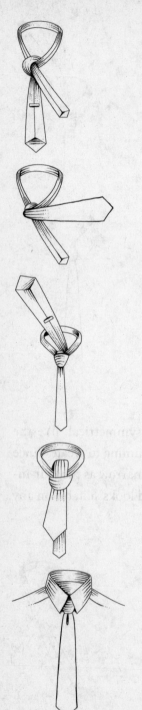

2. Cross the two ends over to form an X and flip the fat end up and through the loop to form a knot around the smaller end.

3. Pull both ends apart quite tightly to ensure your knot is snug, then bring the fat end of the tie over the thin end to cover your first knot.

4. Pull the fat end up and through the loop, then drop it down through the knot.

5. Tighten and dimple up.

TIE TYING TIPS

■ Don't leave yourself less than five or ten minutes to tie your tie. Give yourself enough time to properly tie, readjust as necessary, and lock down that crucial dimple.

■ Use the help of a mirror to assist you in tying your tie. You'll need it to measure whether the tie is the right length and whether it falls properly on your shirt.

■ Upon completion of your knot, the fat end should hang lower than the thin end, covering it entirely. You don't want the fat end to hang too low; a good rule of thumb for confirming that your tie is the proper length is to make sure that the bottom tip just touches the upper part of your belt (or your pants, if you are wearing suspenders).

■ When removing your tie, don't pull the thin end through the knot— doing so will ruin the shape of the tie. Remove the tie by doing the tying steps backwards.

Q&A

Powerful neckwear

Dear AskMen.com,
What is the definition of a power tie? I thought a power tie was one that you felt good in. Is there another definition? Is there a particular pattern?
Rob

Rob,
The tie in general has always been a symbol of masculinity, and in the corporate world, it serves to localize and reinforce the surrounding environment of rigidity and control. Add the dimension of a particular color or pattern, and that same tie can simultaneously communicate raw power.

What that color and pattern is varies depending on context. A striped tie characterized by diagonal lines is often referred to as a power tie, perhaps because it is associated with politicians who so often wear them. Throughout the '80s, the solid red tie was the prototypical power tie, because it announced itself so brashly against the gray corporate wardrobe of the time. And it is perhaps herein that we find the most apt definition of a power tie: It's the tie that purposefully sets itself apart from the pack, and in doing so suggests an underlying confidence and an accompanying power that justifies the swagger. The most recent popular incarnation of the power tie? The solid bright pink tie, most notably sported by Donald Trump.

AskMen.com

POCKET SQUARE GUIDE

The pocket square provides the simplest means to elevate one's appearance from well-dressed to elegant. The difference in visual impact between a jacket and a jacket adorned with a square is significant, and so little is required to achieve it: Just put one in your pocket.

Well, it's not that simple. You have plenty of options when it comes to folding and wearing your pocket square. Before demonstrating the more common ones, here are three pocket square commandments:

1. Your pocket square is for decorative use only. Don't use it to wipe your nose; carry a proper handkerchief in your pants pocket for that.

2. While it is acceptable to sport matching tie/square sets, you'll note that they are rarely—if ever—exact matches in terms of color or pattern. This is for good reason: Matching these two elements perfectly appears mathematic, and thus, bland. Instead, match them as you would any other colors and patterns.

3. You don't need a tie to wear a square. In fact, in the right setting a square is often a good substitute for a tie.

Here are your basic square-folding techniques—the primary five in a seemingly endless parade of more sophisticated variations.

1. The Four-Point

1. Open up the square and lay it out in front of you, positioned in a diamond shape.

2. Fold the bottom corner up to meet the top corner. You've now created two new bottom corners: One on the left and one on the right.

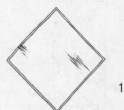

3. Fold the bottom right-hand corner up to fall just to the left of the top corner.

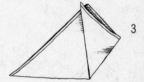

4. Now, fold the bottom left-hand corner up to the right of the top corner.

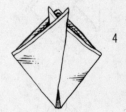

5. Turn the square around and place in the pocket.

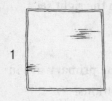

2. The One-Point (a.k.a. The Triangle)

1. Open up the square.

2. Now fold it in half, lengthwise.

3. Fold it again, this time from bottom to top.

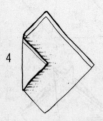

4. Position the folded square in a diamond shape, with the exposed folds at the top corner. Fold what is now the left corner in to the middle of the diamond.

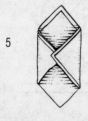

5. Fold what is now the right corner in to slightly overlap the left fold.

6. Fold the bottom corner back, so as to expose the preceding two folds.

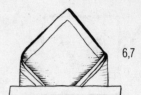

7. Slide it in the pocket.

3. The Square (a.k.a. The Presidential)

1. Open up the square.

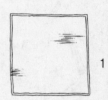

2. Now fold it in half, lengthwise.

3. Fold the bottom up so it falls just short of meeting the top.

4. Flip it around. Tuck it in.

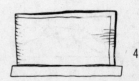

4. The Puff

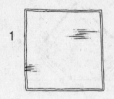

1

1. Unfold the pocket square.

2

2. Pinch it in the center and raise it up, letting the points hang down.

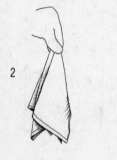

3

3. Use the space between your thumb and forefinger to cinch the hanging square at its midway point.

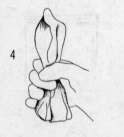

4

4. Fold the hanging points up.

5

5. Stuff it in.

5. The TV Fold

1. Open up the square. Now fold it in half, lengthwise.

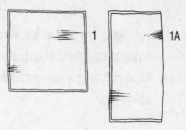

2. Fold it again, this time from bottom to top.

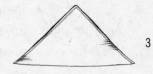

3. Position the folded square in a diamond shape. Pull the bottom corner up to meet the top corner.

4. Fold the left corner over.

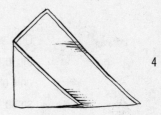

5. Fold the right corner over.

6. Fold the top corner down.

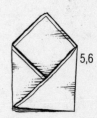

7. You've created a square. Flip it around to conceal the diagonal folds, and put it in.

CUFF LINKS

Cuff links are only to be worn with French cuffs. Don't even dream of trying to transform your button cuffs into French cuffs with scissors. Most cuff links you'll encounter can be grouped into the following three categories.

Chain links

Two studs of equal size are connected by a chain or a bar. Typically, both sides are presentable. For this reason, chain links connote a particular class.

Fabric knot (monkey's fist)

The monkey's fist, a nautical knot resembling a volleyball, is used to hold the cuffs in place. The fabric knot has emerged into both popularity and acceptance as formal wear in Europe, and is gaining popularity in the U.S.

Torpedo

Otherwise known as the "push-through," one side of the torpedo is more decorative, and the other consists only of a plain clip, designed to be hidden. Derided by some fashion snoots as an "Americanization" of the accessory.

BELTS 101

Although it has yet to be explicitly stated, one style lesson that you've probably already picked up from this book is that no element of your wardrobe goes unnoticed. Even that most utilitarian of accessories, the belt, can't be donned without some prior consideration.

There are just two types of belts you must know: Casual and formal. And the best way to remember these two is to use a rule of thumb—literally.

If the belt is about as wide as your thumb, it's a dress belt. If it's significantly wider, it's casual. Dress belts also usually sport a glossy, reflective finish, while casual belts are more often found in flat, muted shades and textures. To cover all your fashion bases, try to own at least one of each.

Three main colors

Picking out a belt color is also pretty straightforward, as there are only three hues you should be concerned with: black, brown, and tan. In an ideal world, you would own casual and dress belts in all three colors. In the real world, most can make do with a thin black dress belt, and a wide brown or tan casual belt.

There are, indeed, colored cloth or canvas belts also available. Bright belt colors are fine if you're a teenager, a yachter, or a superhero, but for everyone else, they're a fleeting trend.

Types of belt skins

Here is where picking out a belt gets a wee bit complicated.

Calfskin

Nearly all belts you'll find in department stores and men's boutiques will be some variation of calfskin. Don't let their universality get you down,

111

though. Belt makers find calfskin quite versatile; it allows for smooth, shiny dress belts as well as wide, thick cuts for casual numbers.

Ostrich

Arguably the most exotic belt leather, ostrich skin resembles uneven terrain, with craggy features and pockmarks from where the bird wore its feathers. Because they're not for everyone, and they take some legwork to track down, ostrich leather belts can cost a few hundred dollars a pop. These belts' one-of-a-kind look demands that their wearers possess supreme fashion confidence.

Lizard

Now you're getting into the really expensive belts. Lizard skin belts, and their even more upscale crocodile and alligator skin cousins, can cost up to $1,000. This leather is marked by its small, dense scale patterns. The look is one of refined exoticism—a more upscale version of ostrich skin.

Keep in mind that belts should be an accessory, and not the centerpiece of your wardrobe. So though you may dream of turning heads with a lizard skin around your waist, don't get suckered into buying a belt that's more expensive than your shoes or—God forbid—your suit.

Buying belts

All quality department stores have a decent-sized belt rack that you'll want to check out. Each belt will have a tag on it indicating its size. Take your waist size, and remember to go one size bigger. This way, your "33" or "34" waist translates into a "36–40" belt size.

Anywhere between $30 and $100 is a good price to pay for a belt.

Matching belts to your wardrobe

The simplest rule when it comes to wearing a dress belt is that it should always match your shoes in color and finish. Shiny black shoes demand a shiny black belt. Simple.

Casual belts allow you quite a bit more flexibility. Whether black, brown, or tan, a casual belt with a dull, matte finish goes reasonably well with jeans and sneakers. If you're wearing casual leather shoes, approximate the rule for dress belts and match your belt's color tone with that of what's on your feet.

Storing belts

If you've gone out and invested $100+ on a dressy belt, you might also want to take some steps to protect your purchase. Belts should always hang vertically and away from sunlight, so as not to dry out and damage the leather. Many men get into the habit of simply leaving their belts in their pants, but keeping belts in this loop for long periods of time will curve the leather and damage its seams. Invest in a belt rack, or simply clear room on your tie rack.

BASIC BELT NO-NOS

Here are a few basic, easy to remember "don'ts" when it comes to picking out a belt.

- Leave the garish, extra-large buckles to the hipsters.

- Leave the metal-studded, S&M-style belts to the surly goths.

- Never wear a dress belt with jeans; never wear a casual belt with dress slacks.

- Never be caught wearing a shirt tucked into your pants without a belt.

■ Never wear a belt with a hole that you've punched out yourself. If your waistline is expanding, buy a bigger belt.

A SCARF FOR EVERY OCCASION

Winter provides plenty of great opportunities to accessorize. And as the style-savvy man moves through multiple winters, he accumulates numerous cold-weather coats to match—or potentially mismatch— accessories with.

The wide variety of available scarf colors and patterns makes them tricky to pair with jackets. Furthermore, they need to complement your coat in terms of style and texture. You don't want to be caught on the slopes in your puffy down jacket and lightweight, silk Hermès scarf; that's like trying to mix oil and water.

To avoid any winter-wear embarrassment, here are some coat/scarf combos for every occasion in a man's life.

Weekend

When you're in laidback mode during the chilly season, your outfit doesn't end with your jeans; you're obviously going to be sporting a stylish casual winter jacket and accompanying accessories to brave the winter cold. If you're wearing a casual shearling aviator jacket (classic shearling is made from a luxuriously warm sheep or lambskin pelt that has been sheared to a uniform depth, although these days you can find faux shearling just about anywhere), a merino wool scarf is the perfect neck-warming addition. The fabric and the multi-stripe design exude casual, and they'll have you looking pretty darn good, too.

How to tie it: Double flip; place the scarf around your neck so that the two ends are at your back, cross the ends at the back of your neck and bring them around to the front.

Work

For a business-appropriate look, you'll need a three quarter–length wool coat to wear over that suit. A heather gray cashmere scarf, with its subdued color and a subtle fringe, is conservative enough for office wear, while the cashmere adds some refinement to the wool coat.

How to tie it: Neck tie; simply tie your scarf around your neck as you would a regular tie, and fashion it into a trendy half-Windsor knot. You'll only be able to properly achieve this look with a thin, lightweight scarf.

Night on the town

When you're going for a sleek, urban winter look for a night on the town, warmth has nothing to do with it. A leather trim biker jacket may not fight the cold, but it is a great way to pull off a slick look for a Friday night out. Add warmth to your outfit with a complementing neck adornment, like a black and gray striped cashmere scarf. Your look can't get any smoother than with the simple trendiness and utter masculinity of black and gray.

How to tie it: European formal; fold the scarf in half so that the ends are touching, place them through the loop, and tighten the loop under your chin.

Sporty

When you're braving the winter cold for hours at a time, your warm winter jacket is definitely the main focus of the outfit, so accessorize it accordingly. A chunky striped scarf is perfect for sporty wear; it's thick enough to keep your neck warm, it's fringy enough to be casual, and it's stylish enough to keep you looking dapper—no matter how rosy your cheeks get.

How to tie it: European casual; fold the scarf in half so that the ends are touching, place them through the loop, and leave the knot loose under your chin.

Formal

For any formal winter occasion, a black, double-breasted trench coat will dashingly accompany your sleek suit. Add a wool-blend striped scarf to the mix and you'll get the ultimate in elegance and warmth.

How to tie it: Classic drape; simply drape the scarf around your neck and tuck it into your coat, covering the chest area left exposed by the coat's neckline.

Wrap-up

Having only one scarf recycled amongst multiple coats is a fashion no-no. You can't mix that chunky knit scarf meant for a day of ice-skating and snowball fights with your wool trench for the office. So, pair each coat with its own worthy accessory and your outerwear will have you looking hot no matter what the frosty temperature.

CLASSIC MEN'S BAGS

Like belts, bags have evolved out of their strictly utilitarian role to become a necessary style tool and accessory. For those who would like to dabble in the wide world of men's bags, but don't know which one would suit their needs best, heed this familiar advice: Stick with a classic style, and you can't go wrong. The following are six such classic bag styles that can be easily mixed and matched with your business and casual wardrobe.

Briefcase

Briefcases are probably the oldest form of "acceptable" handbags for men. Modern-day briefcases have evolved a great deal since the days of your father's sharp-cornered box, but the classic shape, buckles, leather exterior, and practical interior compartments help make this bag a timeless addition to any working-man's wardrobe.

Carry with: Business attire

Messenger bag

Aptly named, the messenger bag is designed after the traditional bags carried throughout history by—who else?—messengers. Made from heavy fabric and swung across the shoulders, messenger bags have taken on a new meaning in urban fashion. From students carrying functional, multi-pocket canvas bags to urban hipsters with leather bags, the messenger's laidback style will always have a classic casual flair, but today's leather bag also exudes a hint of uptown sophistication.

Carry with: Slick street clothes

Holdall

Any traveling man needs a holdall for those weekend jaunts or three-day business trips. Big, bulky luggage has been supplanted by sleek, stylish holdalls (or carry-alls). Its design

is inspired by the duffel bag, but its predominantly leather exterior and more refined appearance attribute a classic look to this practical tote.

Carry with: Casual weekend wear, business-casual attire

Camera bag

A smaller version of the messenger bag, a camera bag is a longer, rectangular bag that is meant to be strapped across the shoulders. Convenient for tourists, but good for any man on the go, a camera bag is a discreet but stylish way to lug around your belongings. What makes the camera bag stand out as a classic tote for men is its ability to bring a touch of masculinity to an outfit, even if it is hanging from your shoulder. It's a simple style with a whole lot of function.

Carry with: Leisure wear

Tote bag

A tote bag is the modern approach to the classic briefcase. Resembling an artisan's bag, the tote is the utmost in casual business attire. Its basic design and usual soft leather exterior allots it a classic status, while its long handles give it a contemporary edge. If purchased in a chocolate brown or black, a tote bag can add a touch of manly class to casual work wear.

Carry with: Business-casual clothes

Newsboy bag

Like the newsboy cap, the newsboy bag is a classic style that has become synonymous with men's casual wear. It's similar to the messenger bag in style, but its traditional rough canvas exterior makes it a little less formal. This bag style is perfect for the student on the go, as it makes more of a fashion statement and exudes more masculinity and style-savvy than a knapsack.

Carry with: Campus-chic wear

BASIC MEN'S WALLET STYLES

Tri-fold

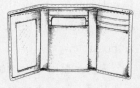

A beginner's wallet in the sense that it is suitable only for cash and a limited number of cards. Accordingly, the younger fellows lean toward it. A wallet for boys, not men.

Bi-fold

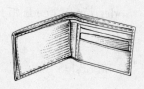

Sliding multiple cards into two wider pockets puts less strain on the stitching than cramming them into three narrower ones would. The dimensions of the bi-fold have remained largely intact since the introduction of the credit card in the early 1950s.

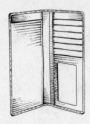

Checkbook wallet

A massive slot for a checkbook creates an equally massive inconvenience for the bearer. Best reserved for those men wealthy enough to have others write checks—and carry checkbooks—for them.

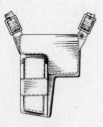

Koffski wallet

This German company's recent contribution to the world of wallets has been designed to mimic a gun holster.

TIMELESS EYEGLASSES

Eyeglasses are typically imposed on their wearers involuntarily, but that doesn't mean that one should shy away from wearing them as stylishly as possible.

Easier said than done: For those with less-than-perfect vision, it can be a little overwhelming to walk into an eyeglass store and see shelf after shelf of frames. Where to begin?

There are a few classic eyewear styles, innovations, and tips that the modern man needs to know if he is in the market for new spectacles.

Frame styles

The core of eyeglass style is the eyeglass frame. The great majority of all men's frames fit into one of the following five categories.

1. Full-rim

Full-rim frames are the most common of the eyeglass styles. The frames completely encircle the lens, an arrangement that allows for a variety of classic shapes—circle, oval, teardrop, rectangle, and so on.

Besides shape, full rims also offer a wide range of structural choices—everything from the style of the nose bridge to the design and fit of the temples (the side pieces of the glasses that rest on the ears).

2. Rimless

Rimless glasses consist of lenses, temples, the nose bridge, and nothing more; the lenses attach directly to the temples. This frame style is the lightest, but also the least durable, and sometimes the most expensive.

3. Semi-rimless

Semi-rimless frames only cover half the lens. A wire or screw connects the lenses to the temples. Semi-rimless frames are medium weight.

4. Horn-rimmed

Now we're really talking about traditional men's eyewear. The venerable horn-rimmed spectacles are surprisingly simple; they're nothing more than heavy, oftentimes dark plastic frames with rectangular frame fronts. The term "horn-rimmed" is actually a reference to the fact that these glasses are traditionally made from horn or shell. The lack of nose pads marks the frame's profile. In light of this absence, horn-rimmed frames may sport a saddle bridge.

5. Brow-bar

Brow-bar frames are almost identical to full rims, but they sport a brow bar, or double bridge, above the nose bridge to connect the top of the frame fronts. As in the basic "aviator" look, brow-bar glasses have long been a default men's frame.

FRAME MATERIALS

1. Monel

One of the traditional metals used in frame construction is monel, a composite of nickel, copper, and iron or other metals. Monel is structurally durable, easy to adjust, and corrosion resistant, but it can be a bit pricey.

2. Titanium, stainless steel, and aluminum

Titanium, stainless steel, and aluminum all offer sleek, durable, and light frames that can take quite a pounding. They're most often seen with full- and half-rims due to the sleek and stylish profile of these types of frames.

3. Plastic frames

Plastic frames are easy to break, but they're extremely lightweight and come in a wide array of colors and frame designs.

4. Nylon

Nylon is primarily used to construct sunglasses and sports eyewear. It's a high-performance material that can be molded to form extreme curves.

5. Flexon

Flexon is an ultra-lightweight, titanium-derived alloy that reverts to its original form after being bent, crushed, or dented. It's very expensive, but pretty darn cool.

GLASSES MAINTENANCE

You can add years to your glasses' lifespan if you put them on and take them off by using both hands. Ripping the glasses off with one hand (as many of us do) stresses the nose bridge and temple joints. And if these areas lose their tightness, the glasses will become more likely to slide off. For cleaning glasses, the cheapest method is to use water and a soft cotton towel. For tougher smudges, stains, and dirt, it's worth spending a few dollars on lens cleaner and lens wipes. Whatever you do, though, refrain from cleaning them with a paper towel; it may seem soft, but it holds wood fibers that can scratch the lenses.

Get in the habit of regularly visiting an eyeglass store to have your glasses tightened and refitted. Most stores provide this service for free, and it rarely takes more than twenty minutes.

CLASSIC SUNGLASSES STYLES

Eyeglasses have evolved into a fashion accessory, but sunglasses have style in their DNA. In the 1930s, people began to sport shades for style's sake, in the 1950s, sunglasses became a part of the beach fashion scene, and since then, this accessory has evolved into everyday eyewear for both men and women.

Here are some classic shade styles that have been worn throughout the decades and are still popular today.

Aviator

Aviators are recognized by their oversized teardrop-shaped lens. They are offered in mirrored, colored, and wraparound styles. They were popular eyewear from the 1960s well into the 1980s, and they returned to the fashion scene in the 21st century with people's renewed interest in retro fashion. Their metal frames are sturdy, and give you a more masculine appearance.

A classic since: 1936, when Ray-Ban issued the first aviator design to the U.S. military.

Wayfarer

The best-selling sunglasses design to date, Wayfarers were most popular in the 1980s, often had a black plastic rim, and were synonymous with being "cool" (think Tom Cruise in *Risky Business*).

    A classic since: 1950s, when fashionable celebrities like Dean Martin made them popular.

Rimless

Rimless shades don't have a frame around the lens, and the bridge and arms of the frame are mounted directly onto the lenses. You can sport rimless sunglasses in a variety of materials, designs, and shapes.

    A classic since: Rimless eyewear became a fashionable accessory as far back as the early 20th century.

Wraparounds

You can never go wrong with a classic style; black wrap sunglasses add a subtle sophistication to your look. Their not-too-bulky, sleek-as-can-be frames are flawless for any outfit that you have to gussy up a touch.

A classic since: The mid-1990s.

While sunglasses have evolved over the decades, each design is rooted in a classic shade style. From aviators to wayfarers to rimless shades, it's best to opt for these traditional styles when looking for fashionable eyewear.

FIND THE PERFECT SHADES

You can narrow down a selection of sunglasses to the classics, but that's still not narrow enough. As with all your other garments, you want your shades to match your unique face.

Here are some guidelines to help you toward that goal.

Rule of thumb

Men with round or oval faces should opt for square or rectangular frames. On the other hand, gents with square faces should decide on more rounded or oval-shaped frames.

Fit your shades to your nose

Wide nose

Rimless and metal frames will fit guys with wider noses best because they allow the nose to blend in nicely with the lenses. On the other hand, plastic frames will make wide noses look pinched.

Long nose

If you have a long nose, then opt for a straight, horizontal, plastic frame with a low bridge, as it'll help break up the line of your face nicely.

Skinny nose

You guys were born to wear sunglasses. If you were blessed with a skinny nose, then any frame should fit just fine. Then again, don't brag about it too much, because there aren't too many frames that will suit a crooked nose.

Small button nose

Men with small button noses should opt for metal-framed glasses with high bridges, which will help expose more of the nose.

Fit your shades to your eyes

Close-set eyes

If your eyes are closer together, camouflage this by purchasing a smaller pair of sunglasses. Smaller glasses will allow your eyes to be nicely centered within the lenses.

Wide-set eyes

If your eyes are set wide apart, then select a pair of larger rimless shades or plastic styled frames. The wider frame will help conceal the wider distance between your eyes.

RULE 7
TIMEPIECES

At AskMen.com, we field endless inquiries about the appropriateness of jewelry on a man. And we always come back with the same response: The only piece of jewelry that a man needs is a watch (oh, and a wedding ring once one is in the mix).

Because it is the only piece of jewelry that a man need wear, the watch deserves special attention—so we've given it its own chapter. But there's another reason why timepieces deserve such consideration. Few things say more about a man than his watch. Its character, look, and style give others a peek into a man's background (and priorities) without having to ask a single question. That is why purchasing a watch is such a personal—and important—decision.

Not all of us are in the market for premium watches. But most of us can benefit from a deeper understanding of them. In the same way that one would turn to a Mercedes rather than a Kia for insight into the nuances of car engineering, the cream of the timepiece crop offer the best insight into the subtle intricacies that distinguish one watch from another. Let's begin our investigation into premium watches by addressing what is perhaps the most common question about the world's most famous watch.

IS A ROLEX WORTH THE PRICE?

Some people will automatically respond "no" to this question. Why? Because the Rolex corporation artificially inflates the price of its watches by limiting the yearly supply of some of its collections (the Daytona is notorious for being near impossible to find), leading to scarcity in the market. It is a strategy similar to the one employed by De Beers, the world's largest diamond retailer, which limits the supply of diamonds on the market to keep prices high (even if De Beers has plenty stored in its safes).

Rolex also meticulously (and some say dictatorially) controls its authorized dealer system to make sure that all watches are sold at its suggested retail price. Any dealer that sells a Rolex at a discount is subject to having his dealer status revoked. So since it is nearly impossible to get a new real Rolex at a discount, you will always pay a premium for the name (thanks to smart marketing by Rolex execs) and not necessarily for the craftsmanship (though it is still very high). That is why many watch experts say that, for the cost of a Rolex, you can get a higher-caliber mechanical watch from a different company.

Then we have the other camp, those who firmly believe that a Rolex is worth the price because it is still a premium watch made with the highest level of craftsmanship. And, of course, you can't underestimate the cachet value of a Rolex. The status and prestige it projects can, in certain people's eyes, justify its exorbitant price. More than any other regularly produced watch, owning a Rolex is an investment and a status symbol, more than it is a teller of time.

SIGNS OF A QUALITY WATCH

Outside of Rolex, few watches carry the kind of brand power that announces their quality through their name alone. Yes, timepiece aficionados are conscious of the weight that a name like Patek Philippe carries, but what are the hallmarks of quality that the rest of us should look for?

The classic definition of a "good" watch generally refers to a watch with mechanical movement. Most mechanical watches use an intricate system of gears and springs that rely on mechanical energy to operate. How do you know if a watch that you're looking at relies on mechanical movement? Well, they'll typically be identified as such explicitly, and have an accompanying mechanical ID (on the back of the face or in the instruction manual) verifying as much. Because of their craftsmanship, these watches are given higher regard. They capture the fine art of watch-making, and command a higher premium as a result.

But mechanical watches, by their very nature, are often inaccurate (when there is no movement, such as your arm swinging, mechanical watches stop and require winding). In fact, a quartz watch (which harnesses a simpler and less expensive movement, using a battery that sends electric currents to a small quartz crystal to ensure timing accuracy) is much more accurate than a mechanical watch, but is sold at a lower cost.

Quartz watches are cheaper because they are not perceived as "sophisticated" by connoisseurs. But who cares? At least they are reliable and accurate. If you are set on mechanical movement, know that most popular mechanical watches that are manufactured nowadays use automatic movement, which means they wind themselves thanks to the movement of the wearer.

Without getting too technical, you might want to check out the offerings of Swiss watchmakers for a "good" watch. They are made with the highest standards in the world. With the consolidation that is occurring in the industry, most well-known brands are owned by a small group of companies. This means you can get the same level of craftsmanship of a higher priced watch by buying its lower priced cousin in the company product line.

For example, if you can't afford a Movado, you can buy its less expensive counterpart by Esquire. (Both are made by the same company, but since Movado is the more prestigious brand, it carries a premium price.) In fact, a $250 Esquire offers the quality of a watch priced at

$1,000 or more. Similarly, you can purchase a Tissot (a trademark of the Swatch Group) at a much lower price than an Omega (also a Swatch Group brand) without compromising quality much.

ARE SERIAL NUMBERS IMPORTANT?

Most premium watches have a serial number, a very important component that identifies your watch and is one way of ensuring that your purchase is legitimate. All authorized dealers of premium watches have access to a database from their respective watch manufacturers, listing all the serial numbers of all their watches. If you spend a good amount of money on a timepiece, you should make sure that your watch is the real deal by contacting the manufacturer or visiting an authorized shop that can look up the serial number of any potential purchase.

DOES IT MAKE SENSE TO BUY A WATCH ON THE INTERNET?

You can get deep discounts on brand-name watches on the Web that you simply can't get in retail stores or through authorized dealers. The main reason is that most online watch retailers buy watches in bulk from authorized wholesalers. Wholesalers clear out their inventory at discounted prices, and the savings are passed on to you, the consumer. Authorized dealers must sell watches at their full retail value or risk losing their licenses (watch companies do this in order to maintain pricing levels and control brand distribution).

The drawback of buying a watch on the Net is that, more often than not, its serial number is polished off in order to protect the wholesaler (who is selling the watches to unauthorized retailers) from being identified by the watch manufacturer. Without a serial number, a watch cannot be serviced or repaired by an authorized repair shop or the manufacturer.

Resale values will consequently be lower, and you might have a hard time getting your watch insured.

The worst part is that, without a serial number, your watch loses its warranty from the manufacturer. Luckily, most reputable online retailers carry their own warranty that matches and often supersedes anything the manufacturer gives you. If you do decide to purchase a watch online, it is important that you do so from a well-established online retailer, to guarantee that your warranty is honored (and that the product is legitimate). If it makes you feel better, remember that most premium watches are built to last for years (if not decades), so neither the manufacturer's nor the retailer's warranty will extend as long as you'll probably need it to.

CARING FOR YOUR WATCH

A premium watch is an intricate instrument and should be treated as such. Too often, people assume that because they forked over $1,000 or more on a watch, they never have to take care of it. That's like thinking that you never need to bring a Ferrari to a dealership for an oil change because you put down $200,000 to buy it.

The biggest misconception when it comes to watch care is assuming that watches can be waterproof. A watch is not waterproof, nor is the most advanced submarine in the world. It is water resistant. Every watch carries a designation on how much water the moisture seals can withstand. Quality watches will offer resistance from one hundred to one thousand meters. Humans can't go beyond one hundred meters anyway, so high-depth ratings are more of a status symbol than they are useful. If your watch does not have a depth indicator, do not take it into a pool or shower.

In fact, unless you're a professional diver, don't bother taking a watch into a pool or sea. They contain more chlorine or salt than you ever want to expose your precious watch to. The elements can erode the lining of the case (which consists of the essential parts of your watch, i.e., the dial, the face, etc.) and diminish the finish of your watch. If you must take your watch into water, make sure you rinse it with warm water immediately afterwards.

Some other tips:

■ Wash your watch with warm soapy water occasionally, to maintain its luster. Use a toothbrush to clean the bracelet.

■ Have your watch serviced every three to five years. Like any high-precision instrument, it needs a tune-up to work perfectly.

■ Store your watch in a soft cloth to prevent it from getting scratched or chipped.

■ Avoid extreme temperatures or extreme temperature changes that can cause condensation.

■ No matter how shock resistant a watch claims to be, never drop it to test it. Shock resistant designations are given to timepieces that can remain intact when dropped three feet onto a wooden floor; take the manufacturer's word for it.

SCRATCH-RESISTANT WATCHES

The cover of a watch's face, known as the crystal, is designed to protect the dial. There are three main types of crystal found in watches: acrylic, mineral, and sapphire.

■ Acrylic crystal is an inexpensive plastic that does not prevent scratches, but allows scratches to be buffed out.

■ Mineral crystal is glass, which is composed of several elements that aid in resisting scratches (it is seven times harder than acrylic crystal). It is generally found on more expensive watches.

■ Sapphire crystal is the cover of choice for premium watches. It is the most expensive type of crystal and is three times harder than mineral crystal. It is made of an extremely durable synthetic material that makes it shatterproof and scratch resistant (not scratchproof). Some have a non-reflective film to prevent glare.

THE SWISS WATCH, LEGALLY DEFINED

Like Champagne, Bordeaux, or Port, certain products have stringent standards (based on location or quality) that must be met before carrying a particular designation. The Swiss have several organizations to ensure the integrity and reputation of Swiss watchmakers. The accepted standard for what constitutes a Swiss-made watch is a Swiss movement, set into its case in Switzerland, by a manufacturer of Swiss origin.

Q & A

What does the term "movement" mean, when used to discuss watches?

The movement is the assembly comprising all the main parts of a watch's mechanism, which move together in order to tell time.

A Swiss movement is defined as a movement that was assembled in Switzerland (by a Swiss-based manufacturer), and whose Swiss movement parts constitute 50% or more of a movement's total value. Movements that meet this requirement will carry a stamp (on the watch's face or back of the case) with the words "Swiss," "Swiss Made," "Swiss Quartz," "Suisse," "Produit Suisse" or "Fabriqué en Suisse." The former three are the most popular in North America.

If your watch says "Swiss Movement," it means that the inside parts of the watch are Swiss, but that the case is not, therefore it cannot carry the other stamps. If the case is Swiss, but the movement is not, it will say "Swiss Case."

Some other tidbits: If your watch has a "T" on its face, it means it has tritium, the greenish-white substance on the hands and numbers that glows in the dark. If the face has the letter "O," it means that the hourly markings on the dial are made of gold.

Q&A

Keeping up with the time

Dear AskMen.com,
Are watches with gold- or silver-toned cases fashionable?

James

James,
Silver and gold cases (or frames) are not simply fashionable, but they are *the* classic watchcase shades. Silver watches match best with blacks, grays, silvers, and blues. Gold watches go with browns, beiges, tans, and other earth tones.

AskMen.com

KEEP UP IN A LUXURY WATCHES CONVERSATION

As you progress deeper into your watch research, you'll quickly discover that there is a very large, and very obsessive, watch subculture out there. There's a lot to be learned from this community—that is, if you can break through their snob shields and persuasively present yourself as one of their own.

Thankfully, we've taken the time (pun unavoidable) to compose a primer of everything a watch novice needs to know in order to stay afloat in the sometimes cutthroat world of watch aficionados. So read on and make sure that you never get stuck trying to convince anyone that your calculator watch is a personal GPS.

Brands worth brandishing

Even though Helen Hunt is technically hot—fit, blond, rich—you wouldn't really respect any man that said that she was his dream woman. The same goes for watches. There are many seemingly good brands to the untrained eye, but for watch fanatics there are certain models that are the Angelina Jolies (the cream of the crop), others that are the Sienna Millers (promising and up-and-coming), and more still that are the Paris Hiltons (overrated). So take note of the brands below.

Cream of the Crop: IWC and Franck Muller

There are great watches that have made their way into mainstream culture, such as Patek Phillippe and Breitling. Then there are those brands that are unanimously respected solely within the watch community—for example, IWC and Franck Muller. IWC (the International Watch Company, *not* the International Whaling Commission) is the only watch company in Eastern Switzerland and is renowned for the elegance and engineering found in its "Flieger," "Portugieser," and "Aquatimer" lines. Franck Muller, on the other hand, is a watchmaker who is greatly admired for his intricately complex timepieces, including "Revolution 2," "Revolution 3," "Crazy Hours," and "Color Dreams."

Up-and-coming: Panerai and Oris

Unlike the sometimes disturbingly young up-and-comers in Hollywood, watch companies that are on the rise can be well over a hundred years old. For example, the Italian luxury watch brand Panerai was founded in 1860, but is only now becoming a favorite with watch lovers on the strength of its "Radiomir" and "Luminor" series.

In contrast to the older Panerai, Oris is a young, nubile trendsetter that started in 1904. Most well known for attaining one of the highest quality ratings in the history of the Swiss Official Chronometer Testing Institute (COSC, see page 138), Oris recently gained recognition for becoming the official watch of the BMW Williams Formula 1 team.

Overrated: Tag Heuer and Movado

If you spent enough money, you could probably get plenty of people to think that clams were great watches. Many aficionados feel that that's how Tag Heuer and Movado have powered their image as elite watchmakers. Chided by many watch lovers as grossly overrated, the recognition these companies reap is usually attributed to their marketing campaigns: Tag having paid massive sums to have the likes of Tiger Woods sport their line, and Movado having glossed over the astronomical price tag of their quartz watches with glitzy advertisements.

WATCH THE LINGO

Anyone who has seen *Back to the Future* knows that timekeeping is a tricky process that requires a whole world of jargon to explain its inner workings. With this in mind, it is imperative that visitors to the realm of luxury watches arm themselves with the terms and lingo needed to communicate. Here is some crucial terminology you need to know.

Aperture

Small opening in the dial that displays certain information such as date, day, month, or moon phase.

Automatic Movement

The mechanical movement in a self-winding watch. A weight (the rotor) turns by the motion of your arm and winds the mainspring. The energy generated by this spring is transferred into mechanical energy that creates the movement. These watches can be shaken or manually wound if the power reserve runs out.

Bezel

The ring around the top of the watch face. Generally holds the glass or crystal in place. In some watches, rotating bezels rotate either clockwise, counterclockwise, or both to assist in calculations.

Caseback

The bottom of the watch, the caseback is the part that lies against your skin.

Chronograph

A type of watch that has both timekeeping and stopwatch functions. There are different types of chronographs available, namely analog chronographs (the old style with separate hands) and digital chronographs (watches with electronic displays).

A CLOSER LOOK AT CHRONOMETERS AND CHRONOGRAPHS

Chronometer is a designation given to a watch that has the highest standard of precision. The designation is given to automatic and mechanical movement watches, not those that run with quartz movement. A watch carrying the chronometer certification has passed vigorous tests demanded by the COSC.

A chronometer's mechanical movement is close to perfection, so the time it displays is almost always accurate (unlike other self-winding or automatic watches), and therefore carries a premium price over non-chronometer watches.

A chronograph designation is often confused with a chronometer one, though they are completely different. A chronograph is basically a watch with stopwatch capabilities. It displays different counters or mechanisms for measuring elapsed time. Counters can register seconds, minutes, and hours.

COSC

In the same way that the pharmaceutical industry has the FDA, watchmakers have their products approved by the COSC, or Swiss Official Chronometer Testing Institute (the acronym represents the French name), to show they are of good quality. Though it isn't required, big-name watchmakers pride themselves on having the COSC test their products for 15 days, in five positions, and at three different temperatures to receive a unique serial number (whose digits correspond to the quality of the timepiece) and the right to officially call their watch a chronometer.

Baselworld

Every spring, watch retailers and wholesalers from all over the world return to their "breeding ground" in Basel, Switzerland, where they are privy to the latest trends and products for the coming year.

The Swatch Group

The largest watch company in the world, the Swatch Group houses some of the most famous, but not necessarily reputable, watch brands on the planet, including Breguet, Blancpain, Omega, and Jaquet-Droz.

RULE 8
THE SUIT

The man's suit is the intersection of multiple fits, easily overlooked details, and substantial expense, making it a rather intimidating first-time purchase. Approach it haphazardly, and run the very real risk of spending a lot of money on something that makes you look silly. Arm yourself with the requisite knowledge, and you will emerge from your shopping excursion looking sharper and more dapper than ever before. A well-fitted, stylish suit exudes class, confidence, sophistication, and all those other great qualities of yours that you should put on display. And the notion that women love a man in a suit? Well, that's one of those clichés that's a cliché for a reason.

With the knowledge of proper fit that you acquired in our first chapter, you are already in a better position than most to brave the world of suit browsing. Let's help you hone your skills further.

BUYING A SUIT: A SHOPPER'S GUIDE

While almost every man would like to have his suits tailor-made, it isn't always feasible. Pricing is usually a deciding factor, so many of us are left purchasing suits off-the-rack.

Now, buying a ready-to-wear suit isn't a bad thing. Prices are usually very reasonable, and you'll get to choose from the latest styles.

On the flip side, many mass-produced suits aren't up to par in terms of quality and fit—all the more reason to follow this step-by-step guide and learn exactly what to look for the next time you're shopping for an off-the-rack suit. Make sure you feel comfortable with your salesman and don't hesitate to ask questions; after all, a suit should serve you for many years.

CHOOSING THE FABRIC

Fabric is the first thing you would pick out for a tailor-made suit, so why not do the same with your ready-to-wear suit? Depending on the season, the most appropriate suit fabrics will differ, but there are yearly staples, like wool, that will accommodate your style needs all year long.

Here are four of the most common suit fabrics.

Common fabrics

1. Wool

The majority of modern suits are made of wool. It is the most versatile fabric, is the best in comfort, is wrinkle-resistant, and has greater longevity than most. Another characteristic that makes wool an ideal suit fabric is its ability to absorb moisture, so even when you're forced to sport a suit on the hottest of days, it'll keep you cool. The most common types of wool suits are merino, cashmere, and angora.

Best season: All year long

2. Flannel

Flannel isn't quite as popular as it used to be because it's a heavy fabric that doesn't breathe much, which means that you'll be kept toasty warm in any climate. Its wear has also declined because the fabric begins to pill over time.

Best season: Winter

3. Cotton

Cotton is a durable fabric found in most American suits; it doesn't quite fit Europeans' fancy. Like wool, cotton can absorb sweat and keep you cool throughout most months. And as a huge bonus, the fabric is quite practical and easy to maintain as it's machine-washable.

Best season: Spring, summer, fall

4. Linen

Linen may look cool while on a tropical vacation, but it has many drawbacks that don't necessarily fit into the modern man's day-to-day life. A linen suit is lightweight and will keep you very cool in the warmer months, but its downfall is that it creases very easily.

Best season: Summer

SUIT THREAD COUNTS

Thread counts are often attributed to linens, but many fail to realize that suits too benefit from a high thread count. The thread count of a suit not only determines its price (the higher the thread count, the more expensive it obviously is), but it also determines the quality and level of comfort of the fabric. First and foremost, it is important to note that in the world of suiting, thread count is referred to as the "Super" number.

The finest "Supers" (in the range of 450) are extremely delicate and should be avoided by those who can't afford to replace their suits every year. For a more practical approach to suit-buying, men should stick to wool suits with a count in the low hundreds. They're the most durable and provide quite a comfortable feel.

Picking a fabric is but the first in a series of many choices that face the suit shopper. You have to be prepared to make these choices confidently, otherwise you risk being pressured into making a quick and misinformed one in-store or, worse still, neglect making them at all—and unwittingly let someone else make them for you.

Here are some suit questions to answer before you step into the store.

Single or double-breasted?

The two sides of a double-breasted jacket overlap at the front closing. There'll typically be two vertical rows of buttons, only one of which has a corresponding set of buttonholes.

A single-breasted jacket has only one set of buttons, and no overlap at the front closing. Well, technically there is a slight overlap—an inch or so. But this is not a defining characteristic, as the four- to six-inch overlap in the double-breasted jacket is.

The classic, simple look of the single-breasted jacket makes it the more versatile and fashionable of the two styles, and the better choice for the first-time suit buyer. But the air of elegance and refinement that a double-breasted suit projects inevitably earns it a place in most men's wardrobes. Note, however, that a double-breasted jacket emphasizes the width of the chest, and can thus make short, stout men look shorter and stouter. This same emphasis on width makes double-breasted jackets ideal for tall, lanky men.

Peak or notch lapels?

The split in the lapels, located roughly alongside your shirt collar, is called the gorge. When the space here is a narrow one, and the surrounding fabric is cut on an upward slant, you're looking at peak lapels. When the space is a broader one, more closely resembling a triangle, you're looking at notch lapels.

Peak lapels are usually found on double-breasted suits or tuxedos, but are increasingly appearing on single-breasted jackets—a fashion forward look that may prove to be a fleeting one. As the type of lapel is typically dictated by the jacket itself, it shouldn't be a governing factor in your purchase, but simply an element to be conscious of.

2-, 3-, or 4-button?

Again, the style here is typically dictated by the suit, rather than added on as a car option might be. Most double-breasted suits are 3-button, occasionally 4-button. Most single breasted are 2-, occasionally 3-, and sometimes just 1-button. Stick with the classics: Go 3-button for double-breasted and 2-button for single.

Single, double, or no vents?

Vents are the vertical slits in the back of the jacket. Ventless jackets are the cleanest and dressiest in appearance, but not terribly convenient: The wearer needs to bundle them up to access his pockets. The single, centered vent offers more in the way of maneuverability, but your jacket will still hike up and look awkward whenever you go for your pockets.

Double vents (also known as side vents) are the most practical, especially graceful and stylish, and, unfortunately, the most expensive to make—which limits their availability. As mentioned in our first rule, the heftier fellow will want to steer clear of them, as they have a tendency to accentuate larger backsides.

Pleats or no pleats?

Pleats are the vertical creases that run down the entire length of a pant's front. Men's fashion continues to move further and further away from them. They do still exist in lighter incarnations, and can be flattering to heavier men. You skinny guys should opt for flat-front (i.e., no pleats) whenever you can.

Cuffs or no cuffs?

Cuffs add weight to a bottom of a pant, helping it to hang properly. They're well suited to taller fellows, but less so to shorter ones, as they visually shorten the leg length. Also known as turn-ups or PTUs (permanent turn-ups) among the Savile Row snoots.

SIGNS OF A GOOD SUIT

In guiding you through the signs of a good dress shirt, we established the importance of being able to recognize such hallmarks in the untrustworthy retail environment. When shopping for a suit, your financial investment increases considerably, meaning that fluency in the details of quality is all the more imperative. Here are some indicators that a suit is indeed as premium as the salesman bills it to be.

Surgeon's cuffs

In many suits, the buttons on the cuffs are simply decorative; they don't actually work. In finer suits, they do. The term refers to their intent: to allow the wearer, presumably a surgeon, to unbutton and roll them up before plunging his hands into a pile of steaming intestines.

Horn buttons

Fine suits are fine throughout, right down to buttons made of horn. Cheaper suits employ plastic, as cheap things tend to do.

Hand stitching

The true sticklers for quality will insist that all of the stitching in a suit be done by hand. Equally wealthy but less uptight parties will insist only that the visible stitching and that securing the moving parts (armholes, shoulder, and collar) be done by hand. This less fussy route is still a high-priced one.

Double-besomed pockets

This inset pocket boasts a thin additional layer of fabric on either side of its opening. When coupled with pocket flaps, the double besom allows the wearer to tuck in the flaps of his pockets without looking sloppy in doing so.

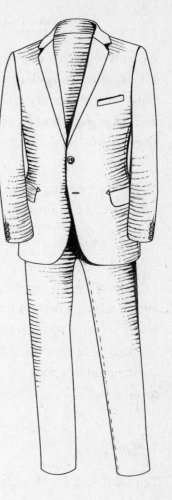

Rolling lapels

The fold of the lapel is not straight and sharp, but soft and undulating, like the ocean lapping at the shore or dollar bills gently tumbling out of your checking account. It's a rolling lapel, and the product of elastic, handsewn interlining.

WHICH SUITS TO BUY FIRST

We truly wish that all AskMen.com readers had the luxury of running out and purchasing all of the suits they needed for life in one fell swoop. Unfortunately, lottery winners are few and far between, and because most of us only buy a suit every couple of years, two rules come into play:

1. Start buying suits early (if you leave college with two in the closet, you're ahead of the game).

2. Be strategic in the order in which you purchase your suits.

To clarify this second point: You need to approach suits as investments, focusing first on those that you will get the most mileage out of before allowing yourself the luxury of straying off the beaten path.

So here is your investment guide. Because suit fabrics are explored elsewhere in this book, we will focus on the colors that you should progress through:

1. Navy

You want to go with a navy suit first because it is the most versatile. Navy lends itself to all manner of formal affairs: job interviews, weddings, even funerals (but wear one here carefully). Go solid colored and single-breasted.

2. Charcoal

Less versatile than navy, but quite versatile nevertheless. With a navy and a charcoal in your closet and a nice mix of shirts and ties to match them with, you can sustain the illusion of suit variety for a long time. Again, solid colored and single-breasted is the smart play.

3. Light-colored

Preferably, light brown or khaki, but if these colors do not complement you, go for a light gray. This is the suit that you can wear in the summertime to dress down a formal look. And if you're the kind of guy who can pull off a double-breasted look, now's the time to do it.

4. Black

Although the black suit is a logical first suit for a young man to purchase, its use is in fact rather limited. But it looks pretty sharp, and on certain occasions nothing else will do, so it deserves to be on this list. Stick with single-breasted.

SUIT FAUX PAS

Since the suit serves as the foundation of formal menswear, you should be very careful not to break these sacred rules when donning one.

A suit is a suit

Do not construct a suit from a sports coat and a pair of pants of the same color. A suit is a set of clothing purchased together. If you just stick any old pair of black pants with any old black sports coat, the colors, although technically the same, will never match properly. Even if you believe the outfit you've created looks okay, anyone savvy about fashion will likely be able to tell you're not wearing a suit simply because the pieces just don't go together. An easy solution to this problem exists: If you need a suit, buy a suit.

Get the right outerwear

Do not wear the same coat with a suit that you would wear with a T-shirt and jeans. Few things look more ridiculous than a man wearing a suit with a windbreaker. If you will be wearing a suit in cold or inclement weather, you should purchase an overcoat or trench that can be comfortably worn over it. The three quarter–length overcoat has become quite popular these days and looks great with a suit. Try to select an over-coat in a neutral color so that it'll go with most of the suits in your wardrobe.

Keep the ties regular

Do not try to be clever by wearing a bow tie or a shoestring "cowboy" tie. Bow ties are obviously fine for tuxedos, but with a suit, they are questionable at best. Unless you want to look like Tucker Carlson or Pee-wee Herman, leave the bows to your shoe-laces. As a rule of thumb, stick to regular neckties.

Ditch the clip

Do not use a clip-on tie. If you are over the age of thirteen, you have outgrown them.

Novelty has no place in formality

Do not wear any silly novelty accessories to a formal occasion. This includes your "Beers of the World" tie (which should be permanently retired to the back of your closet). Similarly, cuff links should stay formal. Save the dice cuff links for Vegas.

COMMISSIONING A TAILOR-MADE SUIT

You've accumulated your store of core suits and are ready to take things to the next level: It's time to go bespoke, and have a suit made to fit your body. This is a fairly significant style step, and one best postponed until after you're quite secure in your fluency in all things suit-related. Furthermore, going bespoke isn't always the most stylish route, for the simple reason that the cut is based on your own frame, which isn't necessarily the most stylish one.

But there's no denying the cachet of a custom-made suit. And given that the goal of the present book is to guide you in all style matters, let's take an initial foray into the tailoring process. We'll start by looking at finding the right man for the job.

"The only man who behaved sensibly was my tailor; he took my measurement anew every time he saw me, while all the rest went on with their old measurements and expected them to fit me."

—George Bernard Shaw

HOW TO FIND A TAILOR

How do you find a great tailor who can tackle creating a suit built to your frame, but also expertly handle a variety of more specialized tasks?

First and foremost, don't be afraid to ask around: Ask a friend, that sharp-looking dresser at work, or go to a high-end department store. Once you've assembled yourself a list of recommended tailors, start doing some research.

What to look for

Now that you've found some tailor candidates, you need to make up your mind about which one to trust with your style reputation. The following are some details you should keep in mind when conducting your search.

Experience

Start with this direct and most important question: How long have you been in business? If you want someone experienced, make sure he's not the new business on the block. Of course, everyone has to start somewhere, but do you want to be the one to take a chance?

Secondly, ask if he can provide a list of clients. There is no better reference than a satisfied customer; make sure you get at least five names, and don't assume they're all happy customers—call them. If your candidate won't or can't give you a list, cross him off of yours; it doesn't matter if you've heard great things about him.

Vision

Find out the tailor's personal take on fashion: Is he strictly into old-school, classic styles, or can he do trendy items for you as well? Having your own fashion authority is a great tool to form your own sense of style.

See if the tailor has the same vision as you. Search magazines and bring photos of what appeals to you. Discuss fabrics and styles you prefer. Find out if he is open or resistant to your ideas; a tailor who balks at your suggestions is not the tailor for you.

Making sure your visions mesh is of the utmost importance. You need to be comfortable working with this person, so it's best to find out from the very beginning whether this will be a pleasurable collaboration or not. You don't want to be halfway through a suit to discover you are rubbing each other the wrong way; chances are it will show in the garment.

Samples

The only way to know the exact quality of a tailor's work is to see it for yourself. Ask if he can provide you with samples or photos of his work, and judge for yourself if this is the kind of craftsmanship you'd like applied to your own clothing. Also, browse through some samples of the materials he works with.

Furthermore, make sure to ask him about his style of workmanship. Ask how much of the garment will be hand-sewn and how much will be machine-made. Ask him to describe the process to you so you can make a well-informed decision.

Time frame

So far, so good, but what about the wait? Check the tailor's availability and the time frame allotted to complete various projects; unrealistic, overextended time frames can be a deal-breaker. The tailor may make a great garment, but if you have to wait forever for it to be completed it may be a good idea to visit the second tailor on your list.

Price

Once you've found the tailor you like best, you must find out the most important detail of all: How much does he charge? You need to listen to your wallet, but don't go with the bargain basement either—unless a polyester plaid ensemble is more your thing.

Hand-tailoring is not inexpensive and has traditionally been in the realm of the upper class, but consider this: Who do you think looks better—the guy in a $300 off-the-rack suit, or the fellow in the hand-tailored $3,000 suit that drapes like a dream?

Choose your fabric

Once you've chosen a highly regarded tailor, the next step is to apply some of that knowledge of fabrics, thread counts, and style points that you've accumulated throughout this chapter. They will all play a determining role in the final cost, so you will likely have to make some compromises along the way.

Measure for fitting

At this stage, your tailor will take all the required measurements to make your suit fit like a glove. It's important to maintain open communication at all stages of your suit's fabrication. Chances are your tailor has made thousands of suits and he knows what he's doing—nevertheless, ask questions and provide feedback.

Tell him how you'd like your suit to fall on your shoulders, waist, and shoes. That's the beauty of a tailor-made suit; you won't need to have it altered several times before it fits perfectly. We all know how frustrating it is to have a piece of clothing that falls awkwardly, especially when it costs you an arm and a leg.

Customization is especially attractive to those with distinctive body types. Tall men won't have any problems with short sleeves or pants that don't fit. Chubby men, on the other hand, can have suits made to make them look thinner and more attractive.

Personalize it

The beauty of a tailored suit is that you can add personal touches to make your suit look genuine and unique. Whether it's specific types of buttons, pockets, or a different number of pleats in the pants, just ask and you shall receive. These simple touches will impress your colleagues and really make your suit stand out from the rest.

Final fitting

At this stage, you'll have to look over every detail. Don't hesitate to ask for a little adjustment—you're paying for the suit, and you should make sure that everything fits to your liking.

The tailor will ask you to try on the suit, while he personally checks every angle to make sure your suit is perfect. Unfortunately, at this stage, it's also time to pay the bill.

TIPS FOR ALTERING PANTS

Once you've locked down a reliable tailor, you'll be visiting him for more than individual suit creations—you'll be happy to discover his range of talents that can be applied to make your clothes fit better and look sharper. The most common service that you'll be commissioning from him will likely be pant alteration.

Realistically, you shouldn't have to pay a first-rate tailor every time you want to shorten a new pair of pants. Chances are if you've spent enough money on a high quality pair of pants or suit, the vendor will offer you a fitting and alterations, free of charge. In either case, you'll want to follow these simple yet often neglected hemming tips.

Wash and dry

First and foremost, to avoid any unpleasant surprises, wash and dry your pants *before* getting them hemmed, as they might shrink slightly. This is especially common with jeans and cotton trousers.

Don't do it yourself

Avoid taking the measurements yourself. Always have someone—preferably with experience—take the measurements for you. Throughout the measuring session, remember to stand tall and perfectly straight. Also, keep in mind that it's easier to take measurements while standing on an elevated platform.

Wear shoes

If possible, wear the shoes you plan to wear with your pants in the future. This will ensure that the hem of your pants will be in accordance with how the pants fall on your shoes; since each shoe is different, its size and shape can affect how your pants break. The thickness of your sole is also a critical factor in determining the final length of your pants.

Wear them as you would

Furthermore, while taking measurements, make sure to wear your pants as you normally would—even if it means strapping on a belt and tucking in your shirt.

Do it twice

Oftentimes, guys pull their pants up higher than they normally would in order to keep a buffer—in case the tailor cuts them shorter. While this seems like a good idea in theory, you'll eventually have to get them shortened again. If you want to ensure that the tailor doesn't take too much material off your pants, ask him to save some "extra material" when sewing the cuff (in case the hem has to be taken out to lengthen the pants).

Avoid awkward breaks

Finally, a quick tip for those of you who don't like your pants to break too much at the front. Simply ask your tailor to take slightly shorter measurements, but to leave the pants ½ to ¾ of an inch longer at the back—they'll break perfectly.

RULE 9
DRESS FOR THE OCCASION

As much as style demands a knowledge of what to wear, it also requires a sense of when to wear it. Overdressing makes one feel awkward, underdressing can appear rude and not knowing where one stands is just miserable.

When we think of dressing appropriately for an occasion, it's typically a formal event we have in mind. And while mismatching clothes and circumstances certainly isn't restricted to these affairs, let's focus on them first. We'll look at more casual environments later in the chapter.

DEGREES OF FORMALITY

Ah, the mysteries of formal wear . . . what does "black tie optional" really mean? Exactly what constitutes semiformal attire? While the characteristics of formal wear have changed over time, it's important to understand the traditional definitions of some of the most popular formal wear terms in order to dress yourself for a particular occasion.

Remember: Today's fashion is a little more flexible, so use these definitions as a starting point and then adjust your outfit to reflect a more modern, sophisticated you.

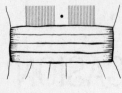

Cummerbund

Formal variations

Formal means formal—no exceptions! There is, however, a little room for creativity, but use common sense. Cummerbunds or vests can be patterned, and fancy cuff links may be worn. Also, feel free to show off your individual style with your shirt and tie color combinations.

Tailcoat

White tie / full evening dress

For an evening spent at an ultra-formal event, like a gala, wear the most elegant and formal outfit—a black tailcoat, black trousers with two satin seams on the outside leg, a white bow tie and kid gloves, a black top hat, a white boutonniere, a white silk scarf, with black or gold cuff links and studs. It's the sort of thing Fred Astaire was known for wearing, and while it's increasingly rare for weddings, this type of getup will sometimes be required.

Of course, nowadays you don't see too many men running around in top hats and white gloves. So, opt to leave the hat at home, and stick to the tailcoat, trousers, and tie, along with the other appropriate accessories.

Boutonniere

Day formal

Day formal consists of a black or gray tailcoat, matching trousers, a gray double-breasted vest, a long gray tie, gray gloves, a white boutonniere, a gray homburg hat, and pearl cuff links and studs.

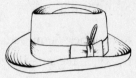

Homburg hat

You'll never actually have to wear a day formal ensemble unless you're part of a wedding party. In other words: Don't buy one for regular wear.

Black tie

A black-tie event is always very formal, so tuxedos are required (for everyone—not just the wedding party). Go with the classic black tux—jacket with satin or grosgrain lapels, satin-striped trousers, cummerbund, and bow tie—and you'll be perfectly outfitted for the occasion.

If the invitation indicates "Black tie preferred," you can get away with a black or charcoal-colored suit if you're a guest, but you'll probably need to wear a white dinner jacket or a tux if you're in the wedding party.

Black tie optional

This fashion style usually pops up on invites for daytime weddings. While party members may be wearing English day coats/suits, and while tuxedos are certainly welcome, you'll look sharp wearing a cotton, tweed, or linen suit in either an earthy or a classic dark color.

Formal

Make sure not to confuse formal and black tie. Traditionally, men sport a complete suit—tie, cuff links, and all—to events that specify formal wear. While suits are still very much in style, in some trendier cities it has become acceptable to wear a suit without a tie to some formal functions.

Semiformal

Remember: Semiformal is still formal. Semiformal specifications can be tricky; make sure the person sending the invitations really means "semiformal," and not "informal," or "casual"—you don't want to be the odd one out.

Any evening event still calls for a dark suit, at the very least. But today's fashion world dictates that ties are not absolutely necessary to complete the look at a semiformal event.

Cocktail

The rule here is simple: Wear a dark suit, but allow room for creativity. Let your personality shine through your outfit. In some metropolitan areas, this look is entirely open to interpretation. Use common sense, and have some fun if it is a trendier crowd or event.

Casual

Casual wear originated with the arrival of the sports shirt in the 1930s. The sports coat was next, and the '60s brought us leisure suits and turtlenecks. Finally, "Casual Fridays" started in the '80s, and offices around the globe have become progressively "dressed down" ever since. Remember, though, that for many men, "casual" actually means dressing up—just in a less formal way (i.e., jackets and good shoes are key).

Business casual

In a business casual setting you want to look professional, yet stylish. The main rule to remember with business casual attire is that you're aiming for a classic look, rather than a trendy one. Try pairing a suit jacket with a sweater or wear a pair of neatly pressed khakis with a tucked-in polo shirt.

Country club

For an afternoon at the club or a weekend lunch invitation at a posh resort, wear suit trousers with a dress shirt or polo shirt, and accessorize with a leather belt and shoes to look and feel at the top of your game.

Leisure

Anything goes with leisure attire. For your weekend wear, go for jeans, casual shirts, and comfortable shoes. Of course, there are still fashion guidelines to follow, like wearing properly fitting clothing, matching colors, and wearing the right belt and shoe combo—just to name a few—so don't get *too* creative.

RENTING A TUX

It's a reality you'll be faced with sooner or later in your life: "I need a tuxedo."

Whether it's for a prom, fundraiser, awards ceremony, tribute dinner, the opera, or that special day, the first question you should ask yourself is: rent or buy?

Age-old dilemma

Most formal wear stores, where you'll find tuxedos, will give you the option to rent or buy. As a rule of thumb, purchasing a classic tuxedo is a wise investment if you foresee yourself wearing it on four or more occasions in the next couple of years. On the flip side, if you're a trend-conscious guy but can't afford to buy a new tuxedo for every affair, or simply don't plan on wearing a tux more than four times over the next couple of years, then you're better off renting—and here's how you should go about it.

Know the occasion

The first step is finding out what type of occasion you'll be attending. Is it a black-tie or white-tie affair? Is it at night or during the day? Should you opt for a classic, more conservative tuxedo, or go all out and choose something more stylish? Inform yourself; find out the dress code and ask around to see what others will be wearing to the occasion. The last thing you want is to be dressed inappropriately. Also, if you're accompanied by a date, you might want to ask what she plans on wearing, to complement her outfit while defining your own style.

Know your timeline

Better safe than sorry; always reserve your tuxedo as early as possible. In most cases, reserving it a few weeks in advance will do, but in the case of a prom or a more traditional wedding, you should reserve a tux one to three months in advance. Traditional weddings require a lot of planning: whether you're the groom, best man, or an usher, measurements for all those in the wedding party (even those who are out of town) will need to be taken, so plan ahead, especially during wedding season.

Know your budget

In terms of budget, you should expect to pay anywhere between $60 for a conventional tuxedo to $300 for top-notch designer formal wear. Keep in mind that rental prices will vary depending on how long you expect to rent the tux for.

Know the basics

By definition, a tuxedo is a complete outfit that includes a jacket, trousers (usually with a silk stripe down the side), a bow tie, and, often, a cummerbund.

Components of the tuxedo

Jacket

A regular tuxedo jacket features satin lapels and a boutonniere hole. You can also choose a cutaway jacket, which is usually worn with a morning suit or a standard tuxedo. It's short in front (usually above the belt line) and split in the back (featuring two long pieces of fabric called "tails"). Keep in mind that tuxedo jackets come in various styles; some are classic, while other models are more stylish and therefore come and go according to the current trends.

You can choose between a single- or double-breasted jacket with peak or notch lapels, and with a regular or shawl collar. The single-breasted jacket with notch lapels is the most popular and classic style.

TUXEDO COLLAR STYLES

■ **Notch lapel:** Features a triangular indentation where the lapel meets the collar. This is considered the least formal lapel style, and is very similar to the lapel line of a single-breasted suit.

■ **Peak lapel:** A broad, V-shaped lapel points up and out—almost like wings—just below the collar line. This is a very dramatic option.

■ **Shawl collar:** A long, smooth, rounded lapel with no notch, almost resembling a shawl draped around the neck.

Trousers

Formal trousers feature a black satin stripe or braid along the outside seams. Because they don't feature belt loops, your pants should be tailored perfectly or worn with black or white button-in suspenders. Also remember that formal pants should never be cuffed.

Shirts

You can wear three basic types of shirts with a tuxedo: a wing collar, a turndown collar, or a mandarin collar.

- **Wing collar:** Formal shirt collar that stands up, with the points of the collar standing up behind the tie and pointing downwards, resembling two wings. Bow ties are usually worn with these shirts, but any tie is acceptable. This shirt often has ¼" pleats down the front.

- **Turndown collar:** This is the most common style for formal-wear.

- **Mandarin collar:** Also known as the band collar, it stands up against the neck and has no points. This is a very stylish, but dangerously trendy, choice.

Shoes

Formal shoes are made from shiny patent leather; they should also be simple (plain or capped toe) and freshly polished. Choose between opera slippers (the most formal option), loafers, or oxfords.

Vest, cummerbund, bow tie, and accessories

A traditional tuxedo is worn with a bow tie and a vest or cummerbund. A cummerbund is a pleated sash worn around the waist. Its pleats should always be facing up and should match the bow tie. Depending on the occasion, you can accessorize your tuxedo with a hat and a four-piece stud set.

WHAT IS A "STUD SET"?

Studs are small pieces of jewelry that resemble cuff links, and are used as "buttons" down the center of your tuxedo shirt. If these match your cuff links, you'll be sure to look sharp.

ALL TIED UP

Tying your own tie is just as important as making the right choice of color and style. This means no clip-ons or ready-made bowties. Speaking of which, a silk or satin bow tie in black with a cummerbund is the classic tux option, but a worthy alternative is a solid black tie and vest.

Colors

The traditional tuxedo comes in black or white, but you can also find a variety of gray, silver, and ivory tuxedos, and some that are even available in louder colors.

Browse the Net

Begin your search online, by browsing various tuxedo galleries and printing out the styles you like. Don't bother with particularly unique or stylized ensembles that you're not likely to find locally.

See an expert

Next, check out the formal wear stores in your area. Bring along your pictures, as they'll be useful while describing what you're looking for. And remember that the formal wear retailer is there to help you. He might have exactly what you're looking for, or he might suggest something completely different. It's up to you to judge and pick out the tuxedo you prefer.

Shop around and compare prices

Once you've narrowed down your selection and found exactly what you want, take note of your measurements and make sure the store has your size. If they do, then get a price quote, along with the return policy details (i.e., when does the tuxedo have to be returned, and what are the conditions in case of damage?). Once you have all the information, go and check out what the competition has to offer.

Confirm availability and place a deposit

Once you find the best deal, place a deposit to guarantee that your ensemble will be reserved for the occasion. It's as simple as that.

FORMAL WEAR NO-NOS

Perhaps the most stringent rules in men's fashion apply to formal attire. This seems fitting. While rules exist for all types of clothing, formal attire faux pas tend to be the most noticeable, since rules governing casual garb are more flexible. Yet, when these rules are well understood and properly followed, a man arguably looks his best in formal attire, as it gives him an elegant, dignified, and polished look.

Of course, due to the rigidity of the rules, any mistake that a man might make is magnified to an even greater extent. In order to help you avoid such blunders, here are some common mistakes that guys make when wearing formal shirts, pants, and accessories.

Button your buttons

On a shirt, all buttons should be fastened, including the small ones on the side of the sleeve near the cuff. Although these buttons might not seem functional, they prevent your forearm from being exposed. A button-down collar must also be fastened. If left unfastened, the buttons below the collar will stick out awkwardly.

No pastel pants

For semi-formal occasions, figuring out what you can pull off by experimenting with pastel shirts and ties can be fun. Pants, however, are an entirely different story. If you are considering wearing some powder blue pants to a formal event, think again. Unless it is a shuffleboard tournament at the local nursing home, you will look ridiculous.

WEDDING WEAR DOS AND DON'TS

- No white suits at nighttime weddings

- No tuxedos before 5 P.M.

- No sneakers, jeans, cargo pants, or shirts other than button-down dress shirts—ever!

- Don't wear something more formal than the wedding party

- Do not unbutton double-breasted dinner jackets

Shoes and socks

Always match

Never wear brown shoes with a black belt, or vice versa. The color of your shoes should always match the color, or at least the tone, of your belt. Those colors, by the way, don't extend beyond black and brown when it comes to formal occasions. Additionally, your formal pants have loops for a reason, so make sure you wear a belt—unless you're wearing a tuxedo, in which case the cummerbund, suspenders, and waistcoat will hold your pants in place.

Formal shoes should be formal

You know enough not to wear sneakers with formal attire. But even shoes you might wear to a bar or to the office might not be formal enough for some very high-class occasions. For such events, you should have at least one pair of ultra-formal shoes that you splurged on a little. These shoes will last a long time, since they will probably be used less than the other shoes in your closet. A really nice pair of formal shoes will also give your look that subtle added elegance that other men at the event might be lacking.

Forget the flashy socks

For any formal occasion, your socks need to be ultra-conservative. Other than muted, neutral solids, your options don't extend beyond very subtle patterns, like tiny dots of a similar shade. The colors of the sock should also match your ensemble; you don't want them to stand out.

Get the type right

Never wear gym socks with formal wear. You need to pick yourself up a pair of dress socks. They should be long enough so that if you cross your legs, the skin of your ankle and calf remain unexposed. Moreover, formal socks should be relatively thin. While ultra-thin nylon socks aren't totally necessary, your socks shouldn't be cushiony or have excess fabric that sticks out of the shoe.

Keep it nice

When dressing formally, make sure your clothing is in good order. In other words, ensure that your clothes are clean and pressed. This rule might seem obvious, but for some reason, the ring-around-the-collar phenomenon still exists. This also applies to shoes: Make sure you keep them polished and odor-free. Cedar shoe trees are a great way to accomplish that latter goal. Finally, if a garment has a problem, either fix it or get rid of it. For example, socks with holes belong in the trash, not on your feet.

Remember: Weddings last a long time, often with much dancing and cavorting. Make sure your clothes are not just clean, pressed, and appropriate, but that you show up in a suit that fits you well and is comfortable enough to party in. The last thing you want is to be known as "the guy in the blue suit who split his pants."

Formally accessorize

Formal occasions demand formal accessories. Don't wear a sports watch or drugstore sunglasses. A fine timepiece is one of the few high-end pieces of jewelry that modern fashion allows a man to wear, so get one. If your budget does not allow for such luxury, settle for something less expensive—but still formal-looking—from a designer like Fossil or Kenneth Cole.

Also, be sure to match metal tones throughout your jewelry. For example, if you are wearing a watch, a ring, and a belt, you can match the metals by wearing all silver, all gold, or all two-tone. The blending of metal tones isn't exactly a mistake, but it also isn't ideal.

Q & A

Wedding wear

Dear AskMen.com,
We've been invited to a wedding and the invitation stated "after-five attire" for the reception. We've never heard this term and were wondering if this is the same as formal or black tie wear?

Roger

Hi Roger,
"After-five attire" is just a clever—and more polite—way of saying, "Don't you dare show up to my wedding in jeans." If the event were black tie, it would have been clearly stated. Basically, your gracious hosts are

instructing you to come dressed in evening wear—a classy suit and tie for the gents and a swanky cocktail dress for the dames.

A trick to gauging how formal you should dress for a wedding is to examine the invitation. Depending on the design, the quality of paper, the tone of the message, and the location of the reception, you will be able to tell whether you should get out that cummerbund or opt for the regular ol' slacks and dress shirt.

AskMen.com

HOW TO DRESS APPROPRIATELY FOR ANY OCCASION

While many occasions call for different garb, not all of them provide the convenience of a rigid dress code. It's time to shed some light on the appropriate dress codes for some of the other events you're likely to attend.

Funeral

Unlike a wedding, the dress code at a funeral is the same regardless of your affiliation to the deceased. The idea is that you want your look to be subdued. Dressing appropriately is a sign of respect.

What to wear: Dark colored suits, such as navy, charcoal, or black are the way to go. Avoid ties and shirts with loud patterns or bright colors. For example, a black suit with a white shirt and a simple burgundy tie is perfectly acceptable.

Make sure you're well groomed; the key word is neat.

Meeting her parents

Meeting a girlfriend's parents is all about the first impression. If you've got a quirky personality, now is not the time to let it show. Let them fall in love with your polite manners and your impressive credentials first, and then let them get to know you a bit better.

Chances are her dad is going to be looking for faults from the get-go, so don't be afraid to ask your girlfriend what he likes and what he doesn't like regarding fashion and style.

What to wear: You can't go wrong if you dress in a conservative but still stylish manner. A good example would be a pair of casual, flat-front pants with a tucked-in dress shirt or a polo shirt. You can choose between black or brown shoes, but leave the alligator skins at home for the day.

Being cleanly shaven is a plus. If you have long hair, make sure that it's not in your eyes all the time, because eye contact is very important.

Job interview

Job interviews are tricky to dress for because what you wear can vary greatly depending on the company and the position. It's easy to come in underdressed and look unprofessional, or to come in overdressed and look like you're trying too hard.

What to wear: If you're interviewing for a prestigious corporate law firm, or for a position in the financial sector, there's no question that you should dress conservatively: dark suits and tasteful tie and shirt combinations. Over-the-top patterns are frowned upon, but a pinstripe suit is both classy and sophisticated.

If, however, you're interviewing for a job with a more liberal firm in a creative industry, the suit and tie method may not be the best idea. For this setting, a pair of flat-front trousers with a sports jacket may be all that you need.

Try to get some inside information from friends or acquaintances in the industry before your interview.

When in doubt, overdress. It is much easier to dress down while you're in the waiting room—by removing your suit jacket, for example—than it is to kick it up a notch if you're too casual. Make sure that you feel at ease in whatever you wear, as this will help you to remain relaxed, cool, and confident.

Regardless of what job you're being interviewed for, it's important that you remain well groomed. No one wants to hire a slob. Clean-shaven or neatly trimmed facial hair is essential. If you choose to wear cologne, remember that, in most interview settings, you won't be sitting close enough for the interviewer to smell it. If he does, that means you're wearing too much.

"Casual" events

Have you ever wondered what it means when you get an invitation to a dinner party or some other event and the dress code is "casual"?

First, let's identify what it's not. It's not jeans and a T-shirt. It's not Bermuda shorts and a Hawaiian shirt. It's not even khakis and an untucked polo shirt.

What to wear: For a lot of men who don't have office jobs, dressing "casually" is closer to dressing up than to dressing down. Casual actually describes a man who is dressed up, but not formal. For example, at a casual event, you could wear a jacket with an open-collared shirt. That jacket can even be of a light color. You can wear shoes that are not black, as long as they're not sneakers, and as long as they match your attire and are the same color as your belt.

Also note that at some casual events, it may be better to wear a tie. As always, if you're unsure about the tie, wear it; if you see that it's unnecessary, just take it off.

When speaking in public

Speaking in public can frazzle a lot of men. No matter how well you dress, it won't make you a great orator, but there are a few tips you can follow to make your life easier.

The key is to wear something that will relax your audience. Even the most attentive person will be distracted by bright colors and wild patterns.

What to wear: Instead of wearing that burnt orange tie, you may want to aim for the calming effect of cool colors, such as blue, green, and gray (as opposed to warm colors such as red, orange, and yellow). You also want to make sure that any stripes you choose to wear head in the same direction, preferably vertical, so that attention is drawn to your face.

If possible, go monochrome. Being dressed all in the same color is not only trendy, but it also focuses your audience's attention. Without any lines or breaks in color to catch their eyes, they have little choice but to focus on your words.

Q & A

Interview attire

Dear AskMen.com,
Is it appropriate to wear a double-breasted suit for an interview? Please advise.

Arthur

Arthur,
One of the first things a potential employer will notice during an interview is your attire, so wearing a suit is a smart (and safe) choice. But a double-breasted suit might be a little too rigid in appearance. For men, job interviews usually call for a navy or gray conservative two-button single-breasted suit. Wear it with a white long-sleeve, button-down dress shirt, and a conservative silk tie.

AskMen.com

HOW TO DRESS FOR THE GYM

Anyone who frequents the gym knows that a vast number of guys fail to wear the proper attire. How often have you seen some guy on the bench press wearing jeans or cargo pants? Worse yet, have you ever had the displeasure of witnessing a man doing squats in spandex shorts?

The gym is perhaps the most important setting to wear the proper clothing because sporting baggy clothes, too-long track pants, or ill-fitting shoes may result in injury. And since you're trying to dress well to avoid getting hurt, you might as well be fashionable too. Many men take their gym clothing for granted, throwing on an old shirt and some sweatpants. They figure that they'll just sweat all over it anyway, so why wear something nice?

This attitude, however, will get you nowhere; the gym is just like any other setting in your life where it is important to be fashionable. You are as likely to meet a potential girlfriend or boss at the gym as you are at the mall. Why look good in one setting and not in another?

Do your body good

Tops

The easiest and most acceptable fashion choice for top wear is a T-shirt. We're not talking about your stained and tattered Cape Cod tourist T-shirt here, though. You're going to have to be a little pickier than that. To ensure that you choose a functional *and* fashionable tee, you should look for a few particular characteristics.

T-shirts should be made of light, breathable material, such as cotton. Avoid polyester. Consider a microfiber material to help keep you cool and dry. Your shirt should also fit properly; T-shirts that are too large or too tight should be avoided.

Don't: Thinking about wearing a mesh T-shirt? Not unless you have a time machine to travel back to 1985, McFly.

Though tempting, you should also stay away from the basic white

T-shirt, for three reasons: White does not radiate heat as well as darker colors, making it harder to stay cool; it picks up dirt and stains easily; and we all know what happens to white T-shirts when they get wet. If you sweat through it, everyone will know about your third nipple.

You should also avoid A-shirts, those thin white tank tops often associated with domestic abuse. If you are adamant about having your "guns" show, just wear a sleeveless shirt instead of a tank top. And please, for everybody's sake, even if you can bench press 350 pounds, don't wear one of those ridiculous tank tops with spaghetti strap-like pieces of fabric that hold it together and leave your pecs exposed.

Bottoms

A wise woman once said: "Wearing spandex is a privilege, not a right." For women, that's probably true. For men, it's neither a privilege nor a right; it's a very, very bad mistake. If you have some medical or athletic reason to wear form-fitting spandex shorts, wear longer shorts to cover them up.

Your best bet here are simple cotton or mesh gym shorts that don't extend more than an inch or two below the knees. These shorts should be worn at or slightly below your waist, not hanging off your butt—you aren't in a rap video.

Don't: Sweatpants are fine, but probably not the most fashionable choice. There really isn't any reason to be wearing long pants at the gym, unless you are self-conscious about your legs. In this case, there are more stylish exercise pants sold by Adidas and Nike.

Shoes and socks

With so many versatile and stylish athletic shoes on the market, it shouldn't be hard to find a pair that is functional and that also appeals to your personal taste.

Never wear any kind of shoe other than a sneaker because you won't get the arch support you need during a rigorous workout.

Stick to white, cushiony socks, or a variation on white. Colored and patterned socks do not mix with the gym.

Don't: Don't wear socks that come up much past your ankle.

Head

Hats are generally a bad idea. They can get in the way of your weightlifting. They also trap heat coming off your head, making it harder for you to stay cool. Also, most people do not wash their hats as often as they wash their other clothes, so they can develop a less-than-savory odor rather quickly.

Don't: Headbands are generally ridiculous—unless you're playing basketball or tennis, and even then, proceed with caution.

General tips

Go with gloves

Weight gloves are a good idea if you do a fair amount of weight training because callused hands aren't attractive. Find a very breathable pair or they will start to smell like your hat.

Ditch the jewelry

Only wear a watch if you must. In that case, make sure it is a plastic, lightweight sports watch. Other than the watch, you should leave your jewelry at home, as it will only get in your way.

Towels aren't terrible

If your gym provides a towel, use it. If it doesn't, bring one. There are few things grosser than sitting on a bench and realizing you are in a puddle of the last guy's sweat. Don't be that guy.

Bring extra clothes

If you do intense cardio before weights, you will sweat all over the gym. To avoid this problem, you might want to consider bringing a change of clothes for the rest of your workout, as you will likely sweat through your first set of clothes.

Wear matching colors

Many guys who manage to wear functional clothing still don't look as fashionable as they could at the gym. You would never wear a maroon shirt with orange pants on a date, so why would you wear it at the gym? It isn't necessary to purchase ready-to-wear exercise ensembles—that's going a little far. But if you are wearing a gray shirt with a black logo, why not wear black shorts with it? It's not hard to put in that extra effort to match, and you never know when that cute girl on the elliptical trainer might be looking your way.

Pumping iron in style

Wearing functional clothing at the gym is important for practical reasons, but keeping fashion in mind is also a good idea. So even if your clothes are still relatively functional, but are beginning to look a little dingy and/or worn out, it's time to purchase some replacements. With your gym attire in control, you can now focus on more important things at the gym—like watching your form or getting Elliptical Girl's number.

RULE 10
MAINTAIN YOUR WARDROBE

By now, you've accumulated enough knowledge to amass a wardrobe that will serve you stylishly for years to come. So what a tragedy it would be if any of these carefully selected garments were to die a premature death because of neglect.

Maintenance may not be the sexiest of fashion topics, but restocking expensive purchases isn't the most attractive enterprise either. You've invested a substantial amount of money into your clothes; now invest some time into learning how to prolong the lifespan of your wardrobe. We'll start with the clothing care basics.

CLOTHING MAINTENANCE BASICS
Practice the rotation theory

Just like you, clothes need to rest. So make sure you rotate all the items in your wardrobe regularly. Suits, for example, should rest at least one full day before being worn again.

Get hung over

Unless you're busy with a beautiful woman stripping you, don't be lazy about clothes storage. Remember to hang or fold your garments every time you take them off. Don't let any piece of clothing lie around all crumpled up.

Leaving your clothes lying about will probably create unwanted creases, and in the worst-case scenario, your garment could even mold into an awkward shape permanently. Hang your clothes properly and let them drape back to their intended shape.

Air it out

Every so often, give your clothes a breather. Doing so will prevent odors from becoming absorbed and creases from taking shape.

Brush it

Dust can prematurely deteriorate your garments, therefore make sure to brush off accumulated dust from your clothes. For best results, use a natural bristle brush on more delicate items.

Wash your clothes

Before tossing your clothes into the washing machine, flip them inside out in order for them to dry if they've experienced the wrath of your perspiration. If left in the hamper, your clothes may be affected by mildew and mingling odors may set in.

If you're machine washing your clothes, use liquid detergent to prevent the development of deposits that can damage your clothes. Separate the light colors from the dark ones and try to wash whites on their own.

If you're washing a piece of clothing with a zipper, make sure you zip it up before putting it in the washing machine because it may damage the more delicate pieces in that same batch.

Finally, if you don't want your outfits' colors to fade, then turn them inside out before washing. More delicate articles should always be hand washed to avoid any damage.

Research stain removal

Before removing stains, especially from garments marked "Dry Clean Only," consult a professional—namely, your dry cleaner. Although there are a few tried-and-true tricks for the removal of common stains, plenty of stain removal rumors are little more than myths that can permanently ruin your favorite garments.

HELP WITH COMMON STAINS

Note that these stain-removal tricks should be used with washable fabrics only.

■ **Anti-perspirant:** Create a paste using bicarbonate of soda, salt, and cold water. Cover the stained area with paste, and let it sit for 15 minutes. Use cold water to rinse the paste off, then soak the garment in cold soapy water.

■ **Blood:** Immediately immerse in very strong saltwater, and keep running the water and adding fresh salt until the water begins to run clear. Rub any persistent spots with a salt paste, and then soak the item in cold soapy water. Do not use hot water, as this will set the stain, and do not let the item dry out until you are convinced that the stain is gone, and have put the item through one regular wash cycle.

■ **Red wine:** Immediately pour salt on the affected area, and leave on for a short while as it absorbs and reacts with the wine. Brush off the salt, then immerse the item in cold soapy water and leave to soak for as long as possible.

ABCS OF DRY CLEANING

Benefits of dry cleaning

If you're busy or just don't have a knack for doing laundry, then dry cleaning can be a great timesaver. It's also an excellent way to avoid anxiety—you know, worrying about shrinking your favorite sweater to the size of your underwear.

Dry cleaners are professionals. They're aware of all the tricks of the trade and can help you get rid of even the most stubborn stains. They are also aware of different cleaning methods, and know which ones actually work.

In addition to all these benefits, by dry cleaning your clothes, you'll also support the steel industry and never run out of hangers!

Minimize your trips

In order to minimize your dry cleaning bill, make sure that you take adequate care of your clothes.

Take the extra time to hang every piece of clothing immediately after you take it off. Treat all stains instantly with water, or preferably, a stain removal product. Finally, if you're wearing a shirt you really like while eating your mom's spaghetti, wear a bib as a preemptive strike.

Save a few bucks

To find a good dry cleaner, ask people you know where they have their clothes dry-cleaned, and whether they're satisfied with the service. You should seek out a dry cleaner with quality machines (these will inflict less damage on your garments than shoddier ones might), a competent staff, and competitive prices.

Compare prices and look for specials. Often, dry cleaners will offer two-for-one specials on selected items and on specific days. Saving a buck or two on each item can add up to substantial savings at the end of the year. But be logical: don't drive an extra ten miles to save a quarter.

Be selective about what you bring to the dry cleaner and use these tips to reduce the size of your dry cleaning bills.

TO DRY-CLEAN OR NOT TO DRY-CLEAN

In answering the common question, "What should and what shouldn't be dry-cleaned?" one universal answer that can be applied: Mostly everything can be dry-cleaned *in moderation*. The high drying temperatures and chemicals used in the dry cleaning process can directly damage your garment or slowly decrease its lifespan.

So, while it may be easier to regularly leave a favorite garment with your trusted neighborhood dry cleaner than to handle it yourself, be aware that you may be slowly damaging it in the process.

1. Sweaters

Dry cleaning isn't a very beneficial option for getting stains out of your knitwear. The chemicals used in the dry cleaning process will shorten the lifespan of knitwear, and this holds especially true for cashmere.

Get it clean: Hand-wash your knitwear with a mild soap in warm water; it's the only guaranteed way to maintain the softness and luster of the fabric.

2. Dress shirts

Cotton dress shirts should only be dry-cleaned once every so often—unless, of course, you have the funds to keep replacing them. Frequent dry cleaning of your dress shirts will deteriorate the fabric fibers and the chemicals used will give your shirt an unsightly yellow tint.

Get it clean: Machine-wash your dress shirts, and then hang-dry. If you do take them to the dry cleaner, specify that you want the garment hand-ironed rather than machine-pressed, and ask them to not use any starch, as this reduces the lifespan of a shirt.

3. Suits

The chemicals, solvents, and high temperatures used in dry cleaning will deteriorate the threads and fabric of your suit over time. We advise that you dry-clean your suit as infrequently as possible (only a handful of times a year) to lengthen its lifespan.

Get it clean: Dry-clean your suit once per season. In the meantime, clean any stains or spots on your suit by hand, using a mild soap and warm water. To get rid of any wrinkles, stretches, and creases in your suit, invest in a clothes steamer. A steamer is easy to use and makes stretched-out or creased parts of a suit (like the elbows and knees) regain their natural shape and look good as new.

SIGNS OF A BAD CLEANER

You may be following all these dry cleaning guidelines, but what good will that be if your garments are being laundered by a bad cleaner? Here are three signs that you need to shop around for a new dry cleaner.

■ **Clothes fit differently:** If garments are cleaned at the wrong temperature, the threads can shrink.

■ **Clothes look shiny:** Fabric can become glossy if it has been crushed by hard-pressing.

■ **Clothes have indents:** If imprints are visible around the pockets and buttons, it's probably because of improper pressing techniques.

Getting clean

It's important to ensure your clothes are clean and wrinkle-free before wearing them, but sending them off to the dry cleaner every time you get a stain isn't the solution. There are many at-home solutions to remove stains and creases, and to keep your best threads in tip-top shape for as long as they're fashionable.

CLOTHING CARE SYMBOLS

How can you take care of your clothes when you don't even know how to decipher basic care symbols? It's a guy thing, sort of like never asking for directions, but it's risky—and can be a major source of frustration when your favorite sweater shrinks to a size suitable only for your girlfriend's Chihuahua. Luckily for us, however, many clothing labels now also include written instructions.

For future reference, if a label doesn't come with written instructions, turn back to this care symbol checklist before attempting to launder your clothes.

Washing

Machine Wash, Normal

A machine wash, normal symbol indicates that a garment can be easily laundered in most commercial washing machines. You'll often spot this symbol on your everyday basics such as cotton undergarments, jerseys, and T-shirts, as well as jeans.

If that's the case, you can machine wash with regular laundry soap or detergent. Also, use the hottest available water, as it facilitates the cleaning process (except if the color of the fabric runs easily).

Occasionally, you'll spot dots, numbers, or a combination of both inside the wash symbol. The dots and numbers essentially tell you how to set your water temperature.

For example, if the symbol specifies 120°F, then the washing machine's water shouldn't exceed that temperature. Here are the most common denominators you'll find on clothing labels:

85°F = 1 dot
105°F = 2 dots
120°F = 3 dots
140°F = 4 dots
160°F = 5 dots
200°F = 6 dots

Machine Wash, Permanent Press

A permanently pressed garment means that it has been permanently shaped and treated for wrinkle resistance. Those garments should be laundered in a machine set on "permanent press." Simply read your machine's instruction manual to find out whether or not a permanent press wash setting is available.

Machine Wash, Gentle or Delicate

Again, gentle or delicate wash is a specific setting you'll find on your machine. Essentially, this symbol means that your garment requires a reduced spinning cycle or gentle agitation or both.

Hand Wash

This symbol stipulates that your garment should be hand-washed only. Use water, detergent, or soap and manipulate with care.

Do Not Wash

The following symbol is normally accompanied by a dry cleaning symbol. It indicates that the garment should be cleaned professionally.

Bleaching

Bleach when Needed

This triangular symbol suggests that you can use any commercial bleach. Always double-check the bleaching agent's instructions and make sure there aren't any restrictions, which could eventually spoil your clothes. And NEVER pour bleach directly on clothes.

Non-Chlorine Bleach when Needed

You'll generally spot a non-chlorine symbol on your bright colored clothing. In that case, purchase non-chlorine, color-safe bleach.

Do Not Bleach

This symbol denotes that this specific garment won't withstand any type of bleaching agent, so don't even try.

Drying

Tumble Dry, Normal

This symbol indicates that you may dry your garment in most commercial dryers, at very high temperatures.

Tumble Dry, Normal, Low Heat

Similar to washing symbols, the dots found in the drying symbol dictate the machine's required temperature. A tumble dry symbol with one dot indicates that you should set your dryer settings to a low heat dry.

Tumble Dry, Normal, Medium Heat

If the symbol contains two dots, you can set your dryer settings to low or medium heat.

Tumble Dry, Normal, High Heat

Finally, if the symbol comprises three dots, choose between a low, medium, or high heat setting.

Tumble Dry, Normal, No Heat

The full circle symbol indicates that you can tumble dry the garment at no heat, or at an air only setting.

Tumble Dry, Permanent Press

When spotting this symbol, set your machine to permanent press. Again, don't forget to check whether your dryer is designed for this.

Tumble Dry, Gentle

The following symbol requires that you set your machine's setting to gentle dry.

Do Not Tumble Dry

The big "X" crossing out the tumble dry symbol is pretty self-explanatory. Use an alternate drying method instead.

Do Not Dry

A crossed-out square means that you shouldn't machine-dry your garment, and is usually accompanied by an alternate drying symbol.

Line Dry

This envelope-looking symbol indicates that your garment should be hung to dry, either on a line or a bar.

Drip Dry

The drip dry symbol stands for "hang dry only" and requires that you don't hand shape or smoothe out your clothes.

Dry Flat

If you spot this symbol, let your garment dry by laying it out on a table, for example. Make sure the surface is clean and, of course, waterproof.

Dry in Shade

The dry in shade symbol normally accompanies a line dry symbol. It notifies you to keep your garment away from direct sunlight.

Do Not Wring

To wring out a garment means to extract its moisture by twisting it. Therefore, logically, the "do not wring" symbol tells you not to twist it or it will shout.

Ironing

Iron, Any Temperature, Steam or Dry

The basic ironing symbol indicates that you can use any ironing method. So take out the steamroller and get rid of those creases.

Iron, Low

Again, for ironing symbols, dots are used to point out the ideal temperature setting to choose for a specific garment. For example, one dot tells you to set your iron at a low setting, which is around 230°F.

Iron, Medium

Two dots indicate that you should set your iron at a temperature of approximately 265°F.

Iron, High

Finally, three dots indicate that your iron should be set at 300°F.

Do Not Steam

This symbol simply denotes that steam ironing your garment could cause permanent damage.

Do Not Iron

It's as simple as that.

Dry Cleaning

If you spot a circular symbol, then you should know that your garment must be dry-cleaned. Have it cleaned professionally (unless there's a big "X" marked on the circle, in which case it should not be dry-cleaned).

TIPS FOR STORING LEATHER

Leather garments can cost a pretty penny, so it's important that you know how to care for them adequately. The most efficient way to learn about your new leather item's care techniques is to ask the salesperson for specific instructions. But we can give you the inside track on proper leather storage techniques right now.

■ Always store your leather items in cool, dry places.

■ Never store leather in plastic bags or other nonporous covers or containers.

- When hanging leather pants or jackets, avoid using metal hangers.

- Always stuff empty leather handbags with newspaper and use shoe-trees when storing leather shoes and boots.

IRONING IT ALL OUT

The first step in successfully ironing your clothes is making sure you have the right tools for the job. You'll need a good iron, a hard surface to iron on (preferably an ironing board), and some spray starch.

Before you start ironing, make sure you read each clothing tag carefully to determine the fabric composition and ironing instructions for each item. Then simply choose your iron's settings accordingly.

Using starch will make your clothes feel crisp and look even better, while cutting down your ironing time considerably. Simply lay the garment down flat on the ironing board and spray the starch onto it from at least a foot away before you begin.

In general, it's best to iron clothes inside out in order to preserve the garment's color and prevent staining.

Shirts

When ironing shirts, start with the collar; move the iron up and down smoothly around the entire area. Then shift down to the cuffs and sleeves.

Throughout the process, make sure to follow and maintain your shirt's natural creases. Once the sleeves are ironed out, move on to the buttonhole area (gently iron around each buttonhole), after which you should move on to one of the front halves, and finally work your way around to the other front half.

Once you're done, make sure to properly hang your shirt.

Pants

When ironing pants, start with the waistband and slowly move your way down to the cuffs (or hem).

Place your slacks parallel to the ironing board and slowly move the iron up and down, working your way over the entire wrinkled areas. Again, always make sure to follow and maintain your pants' natural lines and creases.

Once you're done, hang your pants without delay.

Laundering tips

Before even whipping out your iron, make sure your clothes are in tip-top shape because ironing a dirty shirt could permanently set stains into the fabric.

When washing your clothing, always try to use high-quality detergent and fabric softener, as they will help keep the fabric in good shape for a longer amount of time. By using high-end products, your clothes will maintain their durability, which might also render them less likely to wrinkle. Furthermore, throwing a good fabric softener into the mix relaxes your garments' fabrics, decreasing the chances of them getting wrinkled in the first place.

Also, get into the habit of hanging up or folding your clothes as soon as the drying cycle is over. Take your clothes out of the dryer as soon as they are dry (they're more likely to wrinkle when left in the dryer); this should make your ironing task that much easier.

Be safe!

■ Never leave the iron unattended when it's on because it could tip over and burn something or, worse, someone.

■ Remember to unplug the iron before filling it up with water.

■ To prevent your clothes from burning, place a cloth or towel between the garment and the iron (especially useful for delicate fabrics like linen or nylon).

■ Some articles of clothing, such as suits and silk shirts, are more difficult to iron, and require more care. For these pieces, consider a trip to the dry cleaner.

TRAVEL IN STYLE: PACKING TIPS

Opening your luggage to discover clothing destruction is a bad way to start a trip. Here are some tips to help avert such disasters.

■ When packing, fold your shirts flat and roll all your pants and ties to avoid wrinkling. Make sure to optimize your luggage space, and leave a bit of room for potential souvenirs and gifts that you can pack on your way back home.

■ Make sure the luggage you choose has water-resistant material inside. Many people have opened their suitcases only to discover a puddle of liquid sitting at the bottom and eating away at their expensive clothes.

■ Line the bottom of your suitcase with a few plastic bags, which you can use as laundry bags later.

RULE 11
GROOMING

The metrosexual craze of the early '00s acted as both a blessing and a curse in drawing attention to men's skin care. On the one hand, it's an area that deserves attention. Your face is the first thing that people look at, and some stray nose hairs or a couple of patches of dry skin are certainly sufficient to taint that first impression.

At the same time, however, the emphasis put on this element of men's style during this period was a bit excessive. Whether this was the result of a saturation of product placement or simply an overcompensatory attempt to masculinize a woman's domain, the end result was hysteric, characterized by—dare we say—feminine undertones. The enduring image is of effeminate makeover show hosts waltzing through cosmetics aisles, and it's one that men continue to recoil from today.

But the fact remains: Your face is the first thing that people look at. And we didn't go to the trouble of writing this guide so that you could negate all its lessons by not cleaning your ears properly. So let's start with a brief roundup of core hygiene steps that should be incorporated into your routine.

HYGIENE 101

Take a shower every morning

There's just no excuse for missing a shower when you wake up, before you go out for the night, or after a workout. Water, soap, towel. Simple.

Check your face

Before leaving the house in the morning, ensure that your face is clean and free of "debris." A quick look in the mirror to check for nose hair, stuff in your beard, or crust in your eyes doesn't take more than a few seconds, and is well worth the effort.

Groom your hair (ears, nose, chest, head, etc.)

Hair growth happens with regularity, so make trimming and upkeep part of your routine. Wash and condition your hair every day (or every other day, depending on your hair type and length). Set aside one day a week (preferably a Saturday or Sunday, when you have more time) to tend to ear, nose, and chest hair.

Clean your hands

In the business world, handshakes can make or break you; in the dating world, a woman expects to see nice hands. So all you have to do is cut your nails regularly, scrape away the dirt with a "nail cleaner" or a nail-brush (which you can keep in the shower to save time), wash your hands frequently (to avoid sweaty, sticky hands), and use lotion on occasion (to keep them smooth).

Apply lip balm

There is nothing worse than looking at chapped lips, and no girl will want to kiss them. Find a good lip balm and use it regularly. Just don't put too much on, or it will end up looking like lip gloss. And if you don't like applying it in public because of the unmanly look it portrays, then do it in private when you go to the bathroom.

MEN'S COSMETICS BASICS

Despite what the makeover shows of yore suggested, there is a middle ground between a complete absence of skin care products and stocking a home pharmacy. But there is such a bewildering myriad of products out there that choosing the right and necessary ones can be a bit overwhelming.

The following products are each designed for a particular and worthwhile task, but before you slather on these cleansers and toners, don't forget the most important thing for your skin: sunblock. Though technically not a cosmetic in and of itself, sunblock is added to many lotions. If yours doesn't contain it, get a separate bottle—preferably one that has an SPF of 15 or higher and that is unscented; you don't want to smell like a coconut at work.

Cleansers

Every man needs to start his day by cleaning his face. Starting with a clean palette is of utmost importance. Cleansers are designed to rid the skin of dirt, grime, and pollutants. Men who wash their skin properly can expect fewer breakouts and a generally fresher appearance. Start and finish your day with a good facial cleanse, and your skin will thank you for years to come.

Toners

Toners clean and tighten your pores, making it harder for irritants, dirt, and stress to take a toll on your complexion. These products act like a seal for your pores after cleansing and lessen the chances of blackheads and breakouts. Toners leave your skin looking brighter and feeling fresher. If you have dry skin, use a toner designed specifically for your skin type—some toners contain alcohol and are better for men with oily skin.

Moisturizers

Moisturizers are very important in maintaining smooth, youthful-looking skin. These lotions work by softening and diminishing fine lines and wrinkles. All skin types can benefit from moisturizers, as regular use will lessen the chance of fine lines. If you have oily skin, go for a non-greasy formula. Even younger skin can benefit—why give wrinkles a head start? Apply your moisturizer after cleansing and toning and you can expect softer, suppler skin.

When it comes to moisturizers, take a small amount (around the size of a quarter) and massage it gently into your face after toning. Just make sure you use these lotions with sunblock only in the morning since there's no need to wear SPF on your skin at night.

EXFOLIATION

What is exfoliation? It's the process of scrubbing off dead skin cells to reveal and expose "younger," fresher skin. The shedding process unclogs pores, keeps skin clean, and helps reduce acne breakouts. It also exposes the face's hair follicles, allowing for a better shave.

The exfoliation process requires an exfoliation-specific cleanser/foamer. Most of these products contain some combination of granulated pumice, sea salts, fruit seeds, salicylic acid, alpha hydroxy acid, and beta hydroxy acid, all of which serve to loosen and slough off dead skin cells.

To get the most out of your exfoliating cleanser—and to help work it into a good lather—you should use one of the following methods of application.

Exfoliating gloves

Just put them on and gently rub the cleanser around your face. The gloves' massaging motion will also improve circulation and open pores. We're veering into metrosexual territory here, so don't feel the need to put your exfoliating gloves on prominent display.

Sponge

An abrasive sponge, or loofah (a sponge made from the dried fibrous part of the loofah plant), works the same way as gloves, but it has the advantage of whipping the exfoliating cleanser into a richer lather that gets deeper into the pores and the skin's upper layers.

Exfoliating mask

This is a plaster-like concoction that goes on your face as a liquid goop, hardens, and then peels off to remove dead skin cells, dirt, whiteheads, etc. It can be pricey, and more than a little feminine, but its thoroughness more than makes up for it.

Pumice soap

This is a bar soap that includes granulated volcanic ash that *really* scrubs hard. The only disadvantage is that pumice soaps require a fair amount of scrubbing to get a good lather going.

Note: However you choose to exfoliate, don't forget to moisturize. Exfoliation can dry out already dry skin, but a moisturizer will help stabilize your skin and "feed" the new, young skin you've exposed.

BUILD YOUR COMPLETE SHAVING KIT

Most guys' shaving kits consist of little more than a blade and a can of foam. But obtaining a perfect shave that makes you feel like a new man requires so much more.

The shaving essentials described below are the basics you'll need for a proper shave.

Pre-shave products

Before shaving, use an exfoliant scrub and hot water to open your pores. Ideally, you should shower before shaving, but simply wrapping a hot, wet towel around your face for a minute also works. Whichever method you choose, the goal is to get your skin supple and warm, and your whiskers fluffed.

Oils

Using a pre-shave oil is a must. It will soften facial hair and open skin pores to ensure a close shave.

The best pre-shave oils and creams use natural oils, such as coconut, sunflower, olive, or other oils drawn from plants. Unlike mineral oil, natural oils are low on the grease factor, so they won't clog pores and cause damage to your skin. Also, keep your eyes open for pre-shave oils that contain antibacterial agents; these will help guard against breakouts and painful cuts.

Oils for electric shavers

All decent electric shavers come with blade oil. Use it. It's in your face's best interest. Just put a dot of oil on the shaver's cutting block or blades, turn on the unit, and let the oil work its way through. This will help the shaver work properly and protect your hair from being ripped out by rickety blades.

There are also skin oils like Lectric Shave and Jack Black that are specially formulated for electric shavers. These oils make the hair stand up for a smoother cut, and create a sleek surface for the shaver to glide across.

Shaving powders

There are two types of shaving powders. One is a depilatory powder, which is used to avoid razor bumps and ingrown hairs. The other kind is meant for use with electric shavers; it works like shaving oil, softening the hair and fluffing it up.

Lathers

Cream/foam

Shaving creams and foams are similar, but foams have more air and come in a can, while creams come in a small bottle or tube. Both soften whiskers like shaving oils, but they also moisturize and lubricate the skin. One of their biggest advantages is that they rinse easily from blades. To get the best results from both, be sure to massage them into your beard with your hands or a shaving brush for a full minute.

Many creams and foams also contain aloe to heal the skin and guard it from drying out. The best of these lathers are glycerin-based. Steer clear of creams and foams that contain numbing agents like benzocaine and menthol, as these will close your pores and prevent proper exfoliation.

Shaving soap

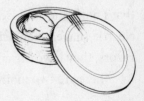

The classic. This is what old British generals used while shaving with a straight razor over a washbasin. Like shaving cream, it's made for application by brush, and must be mixed in a shaving cup or bowl. When properly lathered, shaving soap definitely does the job, but because it's soap, it might dry out your skin.

Gel

Shaving gels have become very popular over the past ten years, as they create a slick surface that maximizes the razor's glide. However, their disadvantages are that they don't wash off blades or faces easily, and they can clog pores.

Brushes

When it comes to obtaining a perfect, creamy lather, only a badger-hair brush gets it right.

As it applies the lather to your face, its hairs exfoliate, massage, and fluff out your whiskers to ensure they're "standing at attention" when the blade moves over them.

Boar bristle brushes are stronger and thicker (and cheaper) than badger-hair models, but they're not as flexible or as soft on your face.

Razors

Electric shavers

Electric shavers are convenient, fast, and long-lasting. Nonetheless, despite years of innovation and advancement, they still result in a shave that's not quite as close as one achieved with a safety razor. Yet, because electric shavers don't shave off the uppermost layer of skin as do safety razors, they have the advantage of rarely causing razor burn or cuts.

There are two main electric shaver designs.

■ **A rotary shaver** has a series of blades organized in a circular pattern on anywhere from one to three wheels. As you move the shaver across your face, the spinning wheels cut your beard like a lawnmower. Rotary shavers excel at cutting longer beards.

■ **A foil shaver** contains a thin sheet of metal perforated with hundreds of tiny holes. Underneath this metal sheet are one to four horizontal rows of tiny cylindrical blades. As you move the shaver on your skin, your whiskers enter the holes, and the spinning blades cut them off.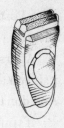

Most fans of electric shavers believe that foil shavers provide closer shaves, but it's really a matter of personal taste.

Reusable razors

Stay away from disposable razors and invest in a quality multi-blade cartridge safety razor or a double-edged safety razor. The old straight-edged razor is best left to the trained barber.

Razor cartridges (two to four blades) give the closest possible shave (next to a barber's straight-edge) and cut hair at an angle. However, this angle and the closeness of its shave can cause the hair to grow back with a slight curl, which can ultimately lead to razor bumps and ingrown hairs.

Double-edged safety razors are classic with a single, well-sharpened double-edged blade. They don't cut as close as razor cartridges, but they still shave well, and they prevent bumps and irritation. Their one big disadvantage is a tendency to cause shaving nicks.

A blade or cartridge's longevity depends on how often you shave and how full your beard grows in. Most safety razor cartridges and razor-blades last between one and four weeks.

Post-shave products

Post-shave products will relieve burn, dryness, and razor bumps, and some will even help heal cuts.

To make it simple, look for aftershave balms and gels that contain vitamins C and E, natural oils to moisturize, and aloe to help heal the skin. Post-shave products with built-in sunscreen are also a solid purchase.

Aftershave is heavy on the alcohol and will dry out your skin. Avoid it. If you are going to use traditional aftershave, though, pat it on gently. And don't overdo it; a little goes a long way.

If you don't want to buy expensive balms and creams, simply splash cold water on your face to close your pores, pat it dry, and finish with a basic moisturizer. If you break out after shaving, stick with a water-based moisturizer.

And if you really want to nip razor burn in the bud, eschew the cold water in favor of ice cubes. Rub one over your face and you'll close those pores right up.

Finally, a styptic pencil is a good addition to any shaving kit. The pencil's aluminum sulfate stops shaving cuts in a pinch. The pencil's only drawback? It stings. If that's too much for you, try using lip balm on the cuts instead.

GUIDE TO BODY HAIR REMOVAL

An increasing number of men now remove sections of their body hair, if not all of it. Some guys do it for aesthetic reasons, while others do it for their participation in particular sports like bodybuilding or cycling. And many men do it simply to please their women.

There is no proven method for permanent hair removal. But some techniques will help you reduce hair growth permanently. Let's take a look at these different techniques.

Mechanical epilators

Hold your horses, boys; these machines are indeed called mechanical epilators, but they don't come equipped with 2.0-liter V6 engines. A mechanical epilator is simply a small electric machine with a rubber roller or coiled spring, which catches hair and pulls it out.

Depilatories

Also referred to as "chemical shaving," depilatory creams are lotions that dissolve the protein structure of your hair and cause it to separate from the skin. You rinse off the cream, and poof! The hair is gone. Don't worry, it sounds much worse than it really is.

Tweezing

Tweezing entails pulling out strands of hair from their root, one by one.

Waxing

Waxing involves pulling sections of hair out from the roots. There are many techniques and products offered on the market. Choose between a do-it-yourself product or have it done professionally.

Electrolysis

Electrolysis involves inserting a needle under your skin in order to zap an electric current through your hair follicle and damage it. By "damaging" it, your hair will eventually grow more weakly and slowly, until it eventually stops growing altogether.

Laser

Beaming the laser on small areas of your skin basically destroys the hair follicle and impairs its growth. It is said to work best for people with light skin and dark hair.

Photo-epilation or pulsed laser

Photo-epilation is a treatment that uses an intense pulsed light to destroy hair follicles. Like with laser or electrolysis, the idea is to impair and minimize hair growth.

Trimming

Last, but not least, you can always trim your body hair with a clipper, shaver, or even with scissors. These methods work best to trim your underarms and the vicinity of your genital area.

ADVANTAGES OF LOSING HAIR DOWN THERE

■ It makes objects nearby appear larger than they actually are. That's right, pubic-hair removal makes your pecker look fiercely larger. Okay, maybe not fiercely, but you get the picture.

■ When your woman preps herself to greet your manhood and his nutty friends for an extended period of time, she'll have a jolly old time considering she won't have to be spitting out hair every four seconds. Best of all, she won't avoid your testes.

MATCH COLOGNE TO YOUR BODY TYPE

When it comes to buying cologne, most men take one of two routes:

1. They restock bottles of the same cologne they've been using since high school.

2. They mix it up, changing their cologne based on what smells good to them at the department store counter.

The latter route is obviously preferable, but choosing the right cologne isn't just a matter of what suits your nose—it's a matter of what suits your skin. The way a particular fragrance smells will change from guy to guy, as a cologne's scent is the product of chemical reactions between your skin and the cologne's ingredients.

How to test cologne

Before getting into the nitty-gritty of matching cologne with skin type, here are some basics for picking out cologne:

Play the right notes

Each cologne is comprised of three "notes," or fragrances. While you're at the store, pick your favorite colognes, and spray a sample of each onto a blotter card (practically every fragrance counter provides these for free). Smell the cologne; this is the first note, or "top note"; essentially, it's your first impression of a scent.

Wait ten to fifteen minutes and smell the card again. This is the middle note: it's the scent that takes over after the top note dissipates.

Now, wait forty-five minutes to an hour, and smell again. This is the "dry-down note"—the longest-lasting scent and one that will hang on for three to four hours. If all three notes meet your olfactory standards, you're good to go.

COLOGNE INGREDIENTS TO AVOID

Many types of cologne contain synthetic compounds. Some common ones that have been known to cause skin problems like rashes, hives, dermatitis, or eczema, as well as respiratory problems, include:

- Benzyl alcohol

- Benzyl acetate

- Benzaldehyde

- Limonene

- Linalool

- A-pinene

- Ethyl acetate

- Acetone

How to match cologne and skin type

Both cologne quality and effectiveness are tied to a great range of factors, such as diet, environment, genetics, and behavior (stress, smoking, etc.). But the biggest x-factors are your skin type and pH levels. And the more oily (or dry) skin is, the more potent (or weak) cologne can smell.

Oily skin

Skins high in natural oil represent more active body chemistry. This extra oil at the skin's surface can interact with cologne to create longer-lasting, more powerful scents. Alternately, too many natural skin oils (including perspiration) can merge with cologne to form an unwelcome odor.

To guard against this, wear less cologne over the course of the day and opt for lighter fragrances, or types of cologne that contain fewer hints of musk and earth, and more citrus and floral tones. Cologne developed for summertime wear is the best bet for men with oily skin.

Dry skin

Cologne dissipates faster from dry skin, so it must be applied more frequently. However, because of the ethyl alcohol base, frequent reapplications run the risk of further drying out and damaging your already dry or sensitive skin. What a conundrum . . .

With this in mind, dry-skinned guys should opt for "winter" colognes. These are stronger fragrances, formulated to last longer in drier, colder times, and thereby reducing the need for frequent reapplication.

Sensitive skin

Arguably the biggest danger for the sensitive-skinned man is wearing strong cologne while wearing other potent skin products. If you're prone to rashes and acne, you're best off to refrain from using cologne alongside strong aftershave balms and body sprays. The potential for allergic reactions is simply too great.

When it comes to buying cologne for sensitive skin, follow the same rules for dry skin, but also look for colognes that list all-natural ingredients free from synthetic fragrances. You might want to explore colognes from small natural-health labels.

TIPS FOR WEARING COLOGNE

■ For optimal results, apply cologne to your throat, wrists, chest, or the sides of your neck (opt for one or two of these spots at a time). These are "pulse points" for heat, and they create the best interaction between cologne and your natural oils.

■ The rule that can't be repeated enough: No one should smell your cologne unless they're standing close to you. If you enter a room and people three feet away start sniffling, you're wearing too much. When in doubt, use less.

ADDITIONAL FASHION RESOURCES

Having read *The Style Bible*, you have all your fashion basics down. In fact, your style knowledge is now far more than basic, isn't it? Just see how sharp you're looking!

But it would be misleading to suggest that your learning is complete. Happily, the resources to learn from are as infinite as the room to do so.

Men's lifestyle magazines will help you keep on top of current trends, as will simply keeping your eyes open. Watch what the little people inside your TV set are wearing. You may not be able to afford the same ensembles that television and movie studios dress their actors in, but you can certainly take some free guidance from their wardrobe departments.

Here are some specific suggested titles to take your style expertise to the next level:

Dressing The Man: Mastering The Art Of Permanent Fashion by Alan Flusser (HarperCollins, 2002).

Men's Style: The Thinking Man's Guide To Dress by Russell Smith (Thomas Dunne, 2007).

A Well-Dressed Gentleman's Pocket Guide by Oscar Lenius (Prion, 2006).

The Suit: A Machiavellian Approach to Men's Style by Nicholas Antongiavanni (Collins, 2006)

Style & the Man by Alan Flusser (HarperCollins, 1996)

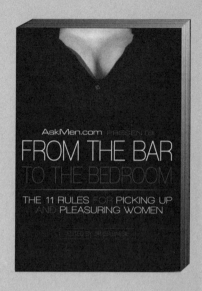